MW01025447

Internal Market Economics is a very big, original concept. An important contribution to the literature on governance, and essential reading for executives interested in maximizing shareholder value or in running effective shared-services organizations.

Don Tapscott, best selling author of 15 books,
most recently the TED e-book Radical Openness

This book is extraordinary! Every CEO should understand these concepts. Budgeting and planning will never be the same in our firm.

Sergio A. Paiz, CEO, PDC Group

This book provides a fresh way to think about financial problems we all face, as well as a practical and useful guide for implementing effective governance processes.

Richard Hartnack, Vice Chairman, U. S. Bank

I started reading Internal Market Economics and couldn't stop. It presents a revolutionary, yet proven, vision for customer-centered, entrepreneurial organizations. This book should be at the top of every leader's reading list.

Dr. Bryson R. Payne, Department Head, Computer Science,
University of North Georgia

*Buy this book and do **not** put it on the shelf with all the other books that you intend to read someday. Read it, reflect on it, argue with it, and most importantly, act on it — your organization, your customers, and your shareholders will be glad you did.*

Harvey R. Koeppel, Co-Founder & Executive Director (retired),
IBM Center for CIO Leadership

This is not a rehash of old "profit center" and "cost accounting" theories, but a bold new approach to making crucial resource-allocation decisions. If any part of your company supports the efforts of other parts, you need to understand Internal Market Economics.

Loren G. Carlson, Chairman, CEO Roundtable, LLC

Internal Market Economics

*practical resource-governance processes
based on principles we all believe in*

by

N. Dean Meyer

INTERNAL MARKET ECONOMICS: practical resource-governance processes based on principles we all believe in

Meyer, N. Dean

Key words: finance, budget, investment-based budgeting, rates, business planning, governance, priority setting, chargebacks, show-backs, allocations, demand management, managing expectations, cost transparency, activity-based costing, service costing, shared services, internal service provider.

NDMA Publishing
3-B Kenosia Avenue
Danbury, CT 06810 USA

203-790-1100

ndma@ndma.com

ISBN   1-892606-31-3

Printed in the United States of America.

To Susan, with profound gratitude
for your partnership and support
in business and in life.

CONTENTS

FIGURES

Internal Market Economics

*practical resource-governance processes
based on principles we all believe in*

PREFACE: What Issues Does This Book Address?

Should you read this book? Only if it's relevant to issues you care about, of course.

So here's a quick list of the issues addressed by <u>Internal Market Economics</u>. If any of these are of concern to you, you'll find solutions within.

If you're a ***leader at the enterprise (corporate) level***, such as a CEO, COO, CFO, or member of a board of directors:

* You'd like to make *budget decisions based on the investment opportunities at hand,* rather than haggling over expenses, or basing budgets on last year's spending plus or minus a percentage.

* You'd like to *manage or cut costs* without causing the debilitating effects of across-the-board caps and cuts, and without disempowering leaders by micro-managing their spending.

* You're interested in *consolidating shared services* to save money, reduce risk, and improve quality; but you want to avoid the downside of internal monopolies (loss of business-unit control, one size fits all, unresponsiveness) and don't want to have to personally mandate consolidation.

* You'd like to *improve strategy execution* by explicitly funding strategic initiatives across all the required organizations throughout the enterprise, rather than leaving everybody to independently interpret their respective roles in a strategic plan.

* You'd like an accurate read on *business-unit and product-line profitability,* accounting for consumption of internal services.

* You want to *cultivate the next generation of business leaders,* and *empower them without loss of coordination and control.*

If you're a **leader of an internal service provider** such as IT, HR, engineering, manufacturing, logistics, marketing, or sales:

* Your internal clients expect more of you than you have resources to deliver, so you need an effective form of *demand management* and a way to *manage clients' expectations.*

* You need to defend your organization from the unrealistic demand to *"do more with less."*

* You lack a reliable source of *funding to meet business expectations,* as well as *funding for infrastructure, innovation, and necessary sustenance tasks.*

* You'd like an effective approach to *cost savings and cost management* that engages your entire leadership team, rather than requiring you to personally flush out the savings.

* You'd like to build clients' *perception of the value* you deliver to the business.

* You want to *change the dialog* with your peers from defending your costs to investing in your products and services.

* You'd like to improve your *alignment with the business* to contribute in more meaningful ways to enterprise strategies.

* You'd like to implement a *business-driven portfolio management* (priority-setting) process, but without the risk of bureaucratic rules or a micro-managing steering committee.

* You need to build trust by making your *costs transparent.*

* You'd like to prove that you're a good deal through fair *benchmarking* — like-for-like comparisons with external vendors and decentralization.

* You want to make the *proper use of outsourcing* only where it makes sense.

* You want to encourage *consolidation of shared services* by becoming the internal vendor of choice, if possible avoiding the political risks of a mandate over the objections of peers.

* You need to eliminate the controversies caused by cost *allocations,* and instead make allocations a fair process that's useful to both you and the business.

* You're interested in *chargebacks,* but don't want to incur the risks (such as clients spending their money elsewhere).

* You need to set accurate *rates.*

* You sell products and services to *customers outside the enterprise,* and you need to be absolutely certain you're not pricing those sales at a loss.

* You'd like to build an internal *culture of customer focus, entrepreneurship, individual accountability, and cross-boundary teamwork.*

This book provides a vision of how resource-governance processes *should* work, and a clear path to implementing practical, highly effective solutions to all these challenges.

SUMMARY: The Contents in a Nutshell

In the spirit of a "drill-down" discovery process, this book moves from vision down to all the details needed to implement market-based resource-governance processes. It's organized into the following parts:

THE CONCEPT: Market economics makes as much sense inside organizations as it does in the national economy. The scope includes all resource-governance processes which control money, time, and assets: budgeting, investment decision making and priority setting, commitment tracking, time reporting, financial accounting, and management metrics.

PROBLEM STATEMENT: Traditional resource-governance processes involve bureaucratic rules, disempowering committees, and convoluted processes. The all-to-real story of poor Robert illustrates their failings: poor allocation of scarce resources, unrealistic expectations, ineffective cost controls, weak alignment with enterprise strategies, lack of funding for innovation, unreliable delivery capabilities, strained internal relationships, slow pace of innovation, and more. Laugh or cry, you'll feel for poor Robert.

THE VISION: Market economics, when applied inside organizations, replaces all that bureaucracy with simple, effective processes that empower internal customers to decide what they buy from internal service providers. They turn an organization into a network of interconnected entrepreneurs (without in any way undermining hierarchical management authorities).

Budgets are treated as revenues for internal products and services, so organizations submit budgets for what they want to sell rather than what they want to spend. To do so, costs are mapped to internal products and services. There are two types of cost controls: internal suppliers must offer competitive rates, and internal customers must manage their demands.

IMPLICATIONS: Things work very differently (and more effectively), including: cost control, downsizings, shared services consolidations and mergers, stewardship, outsourcing, unfunded mandates, management metrics, and the role of the top executive.

THE BENEFITS: There are three types of benefits: financial (such as cost savings and better allocation of scarce resources), improved internal relationships, and a shift in organizational culture toward customer focus, entrepreneurship, empowerment, and teamwork. All produce tangible bottom-line value.

THE MECHANICS: There's a lot more to implementing internal market economics than just setting rates and charging clients for their usage of internal products and services. There are two subsystems: Planning and Actuals. These chapters explain the processes within each, how to implement them, and which of the benefits can be expected of each.

LEADERSHIP STRATEGIES: This section provides pragmatic implementation guidance, including: what comes before what, implementation steps, how to plan and initiate your implementation process, how to select the right person to lead it, and how internal market economics fits within a broader leadership agenda.

APPENDIXES: On the buff-colored pages, you'll find pragmatic details that practitioners need to implement internal market economics.

THE CONCEPT

1. Market Economics *Inside* Organizations

We all believe in market economics — for the most part.

Sure, there are limitations. And we know that markets don't work without some governance. (Appendix 1 summarizes the limits of market economics.)

Nonetheless, market economics is by far the most effective way to channel a society's scarce resources to the purposes that need them the most.

Why, then, do we drop our common sense when we walk in the office door?

Enterprises have exactly the same challenges as national economies: They have to channel their scarce resources to the purposes that create the most value, and coordinate activities across diverse groups to produce their products and services.

Economics is the study of how [we choose] to employ
scarce productive resources that could have alternative uses,
to produce various commodities and distribute them for consumption,
now or in the future, among various people and groups.

Paul A. Samuelson
Author and Professor
Massachusetts Institute of Technology [1]

Inside enterprises, we develop resource-governance processes that fund various organizations with budgets, and we somehow decide what each organization produces. Just as national economies do, these processes determine the allocation of scarce resources to many competing purposes.

But too often, these internal resource-governance processes consist of bureaucratic committees, rigid procedures, complex decision rules and accountability frameworks, and stifling paperwork. It's as if they're designed around a model of a central soviet — the opposite of market economics.

This book explains how to implement market economics inside of organizations. Don't worry.... It doesn't require chargebacks. It doesn't lead to arm's-length relationships without any commitment to the enterprise, or undermine enterprise policies and strategies. And it doesn't lead to open internal competition which results in redundancies and lost synergies.

Market economics simply provides guiding principles for the design of highly efficient, effective, and agile internal resource-governance processes.

These are not radical new ideas; their history (sketched in Appendix 2) dates back to the formative days of the discipline of economics.

What this book adds to that rich literature is pragmatic guidance on how to implement market economics inside your organization.

2. Scope: Resource-governance Processes

Resource-governance processes are the mechanisms by which an organization's scarce resources — money, staff's time, and assets — are coordinated and controlled.

Resources are generated through sales and equity (in corporations), donations (in not-for-profits), taxes and fees (in governments), and debt capitalization (in all).

In any of these kinds of enterprises, there are processes that determine how those resources flow to the various business units and support functions, and how priorities are set which determine what those organizations do with the resources they get.

The goal is to allocate resources to the purposes that need them the most — the internal projects and services that will produce the greatest returns, i.e., the best contributors to the multi-faceted goals of the enterprise.

Put your good where it will do the most.

Ken Kesey

Resource-governance processes include:

*   Business and budget planning, whether budgets are allocated annually or dynamically throughout the year.

*   Priority setting, both during annual planning processes and throughout the year.

* Deciding how to produce things, including staffing, utilization of assets, and the use of external vendors.

* Cost tracking and control.

* Financial performance measurement, including management metrics and the assignment of the costs of internal services to consuming business units.

These processes are of particular importance to "internal service providers" — organizations which primarily produce products and services for consumption by others within the enterprise. Examples include IT, HR, finance, facilities, engineering, sales, marketing, public relations, investor relations, legal counsel, and every function, at every level, other than externally facing profit centers.

Of course, those externally facing profit centers — the primary revenue-producing business units in an enterprise — should also be interested, because resource-governance processes determine whether they get what they need from all the internal service providers that support them.

The concepts and processes described in this book may be applied at two levels: to a specific organization within an enterprise, and to an enterprise as a whole.

PROBLEM STATEMENT

3. The Traditional Approach, and the Problems It Causes

Let's start by exploring the problems that internal market economics can solve, from the perspective of a leader of an internal service provider. We'll use IT to tell the story, although the concepts in this book apply to any organization.

Allow me to introduce you to Robert, the CIO in a not-for-profit healthcare provider. If his story sounds familiar, it's because Robert is nothing more than a compendium of real-life experiences in so many organizations.

Robert's situation was not a happy one. Business leaders were questioning why IT cost so much. They were accusing IT of unresponsiveness. They were grumbling about cost allocations, and expressing interest in outsourcing. And many were developing their own decentralized IT functions.

How did Robert get himself into this predicament? As Deep Throat said, "Follow the money!" We'll start by observing this company's annual budget process.

Robert's managers prepared their budget proposals with the help of their finance staff. They forecasted what they wanted to spend within each of the general-ledger expense-codes (compensation, travel, training, vendor services, capital equipment, etc.).

The managers' expense and capital forecasts were aggregated, and Robert submitted this as his budget proposal. He then negotiated his budget with the CFO, CEO, and his peers on the executive team, doing his best to defend his need for the money.

This traditional budget process led to some dire consequences....

"We're not going to propose anything new."

As usual, the watch-word was "cut!" Everybody knew that they were unlikely to get much more than last year's budget. They felt constrained by the size of their current staff and spending levels.

Overwhelmed with unchecked demand, and believing that their resources were constrained, the last thing Robert's managers wanted was more work. So they were reluctant to propose any new ideas, fearing they'd be expected to deliver even more without adequate staff or money. Instead, they did their best to defend their budgets without committing to any additional deliverables.

As a result, there's a good chance that great ideas and high-payoff opportunities were lost — opportunities that Robert and business leaders will never know about.

Meanwhile, the culture shifted away from entrepreneurship, and toward defensiveness.

[For solutions, look up "entrepreneurship, creative ideas" in the Index.]

"You cost too much (for the value we perceive we get)."

Robert's budget was not met with a warm reception. The CEO, CFO, and business leaders all had a general feeling that IT cost too much.

This feeling wasn't based on a rational comparison of Robert's costs with outsourcing or decentralization. (As we'll see, that was brewing.) Executives just felt that Robert's budget was too big.

Although executives suspected that Robert was wasting money, this wasn't the real reason for their feelings. The problem was that executives clearly saw the cost (in Robert's budget). But they didn't understand all the products and services that IT delivered to them, and they couldn't see how costs were linked to those deliverables.

From their perspective, it was as if they kept pouring money into IT, but they didn't see much bottom-line value coming out. One executive even called IT a "black hole" for money. Hardly much better, another executive called IT a "necessary evil" — something to be minimized rather than an investment that's critical to business success.

Since they didn't know what they were getting for all that money, naturally IT seemed expensive. As a result, Robert was constantly under pressure to cut costs and to deliver more.

[For solutions, look up "value, perception of" in the Index.]

"You're wasting money."

In truth, there was some basis for the suspicion that IT's costs were too high. Consider how managers forecasted their budgets for the following year:

Managers presumed that their current headcount would remain the same (or hoped they'd get a few new positions). They projected vendor costs based on trends and industry knowledge. And they estimated the direct costs of a few new projects.

But did they really need to spend that much, given what was expected of them in the year ahead?

By not asking this question, they missed four opportunities to reduce costs:

1. **Compensation:** Without an explicit analysis of the staff hours required to deliver expected products and services, some managers may have maintained unnecessarily high headcount.

2. **Vendor costs:** Without a link to the specific projects and services to be delivered, it was hard to spot any vendor services that could be eliminated.

3. **Internal services:** Many of Robert's managers provided support services to others within the department. There was no explicit analysis of these services, and which of them might be eliminated to save money. On the other hand, there was no look at which internal support costs might be increased to make everybody else more productive.

4. **Demand management:** Were managers incurring costs to deliver services (or high levels of service) that weren't really needed by the business?

By not planning their costs in the context of planned deliverables, managers might very well have been wasting money.

[For solutions, look up "cost, savings" in the Index.]

"Full cost recovery."

IT continually needed to invest in infrastructure. Robert was able to justify a new data center based on disaster-recovery requirements. But aside from really big capital investments like that, Robert was expected to recover all his costs through allocations — including the cost of additional equipment — under a mandate termed "full cost recovery."

This made IT look even more expensive, and clients fought every infrastructure investment that Robert proposed.

Robert also had trouble gaining funding for investments in organizational improvements. For example, he wanted to improve IT's operational processes by studying and applying ITIL (best practices). [2] But business executives fought that too.

From the client's point of view, their resistance made sense. When they work with other vendors, these are not things they're asked to pay for. And what's in it for them? They preferred spending the IT budget on the projects they needed, rather than investing in the long-term success of Robert's organization.

Being forced to get the money from reluctant clients, Robert had to watch his infrastructure grow obsolete, his internal processes languish, and his pace of innovation lag while he endured continual attacks for what appeared to clients as high costs.

"Full cost recovery" turned out to hurt in another way as well. Being the corporate IT function, Robert's organization delivered a number of services for the good of the company as a whole. For example, it coordinated information security policies; Robert coordinated the entire IT community, including decentralized IT staff; IT managed vendor relations and contract compliance, including enterprise agreements with IT vendors; and Robert and his managers participated in various corporate committees.

These enterprise-good services were not things that decentralized IT groups or vendors had to do. But unlike the office of the CEO and the CFO which also did things for the good of the company, Robert had no access to corporate funding for them. Due to the "full cost recovery" mandate, Robert was forced to include these costs in his allocations to clients. This fueled the fire by making IT look even more expensive.

[For solutions, look up "full cost recovery" in the Index.]

"You don't need all that training."

In the budget process, company executives (led by the CFO) were keenly aware of limited resources. Their challenge was to manage costs within forecasted revenues.

How could they manage IT costs?

Remember that Robert's budget forecasted spending by general-ledger expense-codes. So naturally the CEO and CFO challenged Robert on his component costs. "Hey, you don't need all that headcount, travel, training, consulting, etc."

What else had Robert given them to talk about?

Traditional budgets beg for micro-managing internal service providers in a way that executives would never do to an external vendor. It's as if executives needed to "help" Robert with his tactical management responsibilities, or check up on him.

This was a waste of senior executive talent, taking attention away from the important issues (like discovering how IT might enable enterprise strategies). And in the process, executives disempowered Robert, the leader they'd appointed to run the IT department.

In truth, the CFO had no idea what Robert really needed to spend on travel and training to sustain the IT organization. The traditional budget format set her up to make decisions she wasn't qualified to make. But she had to cut costs, and Robert hadn't given her anything else to focus on.

As a result, Robert didn't gain approval for investments he really did need to keep his organization viable in the future. For example, as is common in many companies, the first to go was training — necessary to survival but a favorite target for cuts.

The result was easy to predict: After years of underinvesting in people, tools, and processes, productivity fell; staff skills become perilously obsolete; Robert had to depend on high-priced consultants to deliver new technologies; and turnover rose.

[For solutions, look up "sustenance tasks" in the Index.]

"We know you have some fat in there."

Robert's managers knew that their proposed budgets would be cut. So they inflated costs (built in "fat") such that the inevitable cuts wouldn't inhibit their ability to maintain their headcount and pay their bills.

Executives, knowing this, demanded more cuts, saying something to the effect of, "I don't necessarily believe what you're telling me about your needs. I believe you have fat in there. Go sharpen your pencil and cut another few percent."

So managers cut some of the fat, but they left some in for the next round. And sure enough, executives came back for more cuts.

As this game played out, there was no reason to believe that the right number emerged. There may still have been some fat left in; or the cuts may have gone well into the bone and damaged the organization's ability to meet its objectives.

One result was clear, however. By building in fat and then taking it out, managers reinforced the belief that their numbers couldn't be trusted. This self-induced mistrust damaged Robert's ability to defend his budget.

Meanwhile, this back-and-forth game took a lot of time, but didn't add value as a meaningful business-planning process. This was one reason why many managers viewed budgeting as a bureaucratic nuisance at best, or at worst as a cynical game.

[For solutions, look up "budget, gaming" in the Index.]

"Do more with less!"

The company faced a tough challenge. Revenue forecasts were flat. But costs were rising due to increased workloads, inflation, and the investments needed to improve efficiency, comply with regulations, and grow the business.

Executives' response was to put pressure on each leader to "do more with less." They demanded that Robert cut costs; but expected IT to go on delivering all that it had in the past (with volumes higher than the prior year), as well as find time for some new projects.

Efficiency is essential. Robert understood this, and for years he and his managers had been improving processes and eliminating waste.

Furthermore, his staff worked hard. People weren't sitting around wasting time and money, such that Robert could simply tell them to stop the waste and hence do more with less. An executive edict to do more with less certainly didn't create time and money out of thin air!

IT would continue to improve its efficiency each year; but at that point in time, things cost what they cost.

So the truth is, with budget cuts, IT inevitably had to do *less* with less. The enterprise would get exactly what it could afford to pay for. Reality is as simple as that.

But Robert couldn't prove this. He didn't have the data or the trust. So the IT department was set up to fail when Robert was forced to promise "more with less."

[For solutions, look up "do more with less" in the Index.]

"It's your job to defend my project."

In Robert's company, each department proposed and defended its own budget. IT was no exception. Robert was expected to defend major projects that benefited the business, with only tacit support from business leaders.

Robert couldn't know the real value to the business of IT's products and services — not nearly as well as the clients who would benefit from them. So he wasn't well positioned to provide the information that executives needed to make good decisions. Robert knew there were cases where he just wasn't able to justify funding for projects that would have really paid off.

Of course, clients whose projects were cut from the IT budget were disgruntled, and blamed Robert for not defending their needs properly.

[For solutions, look up "sponsorship of projects" in the Index.]

"We really don't know the total cost of this strategy."

During the budget process, executives discussed a corporate strategy: entering a new geographic region. It looked good on paper, and the expected revenues were very attractive. But what would it cost?

The direct costs — for region-specific facilities, marketing, sales, and service-delivery staff — were easy to identify.

But this was just the tip of the iceberg. The total cost of a business strategy such as this is far more than its direct costs. It places an incremental burden on support services like IT, HR, purchasing, etc. And these functions may, in turn, draw more heavily on those who support them. Costs ripple throughout the enterprise.

In many cases, indirect costs add up to as much as (or more than) the direct costs. Ignoring them puts the company at risk of making an unprofitable choice.

Robert knew that IT would play a key role in executing this strategy, but he couldn't say exactly what it would cost to implement the required changes and support the new region. His peers throughout the company weren't in any better shape.

Ultimately, in the budget process, the executive team had to make a go/no-go decision half blind — not knowing the full enterprise-wide costs of going into that new region.

For lack of knowledge of the real cost of strategies such as this, executives approved initiatives that were exciting but perhaps not profitable. And they may have glossed over strategies that weren't quite as grand but offered excellent returns.

[For solutions, look up "strategy, cost of" in the Index.]

"Last year's budget plus/minus a percentage."

Toward the end of the budget process, under time pressure and lacking any better way to make the final decision, executives settled on an IT budget of last year's spending plus two percent. (The two percent was to cover a few big projects.)

Of course, the prior year's budget had little to do with this company's unique strategies and the coming year's investment opportunities, or the operational needs of the business. But there really wasn't much else they could have done. Consider this....

The right way to decide an organization's budget is to fund all the good investment opportunities, and not those with poor returns.

But executives couldn't judge the returns on investments (ROI) in costs such as compensation, travel, training, and vendor services — costs which were not linked to any specific results, and hence the benefits portion of the ROI formula couldn't be calculated.

So instead of allocating scarce resources to the best available investments throughout the enterprise, executives were forced to make seemingly arbitrary budget decisions. Wrong as this may be, executives didn't have the data to do anything else.

As a result, the company probably overspent on some functions (wasting money on lower-return services), and underspent on others (passing up really good investments).

Ultimately, Robert was forced to accept less than he knew IT needed to deliver what was expected of it. And Robert was certain that many high-payoff projects went unfunded. Clearly, this budget process was not a reliable way to maximize shareholder value (or the company's goals).

And after all managers' work on the budget, the outcome seemed predetermined. This was another reason why they viewed the entire budget-planning process as a waste of time.

[For solutions, look up "budget, level of" in the Index.]

"My allocation is too big."

After the budget was finally decided, the money was given to the business units (IT's clients). Then Robert collected it up via allocations.

Robert did his best to be fair. He divided costs into high-level pools, and distributed them among the business units based on "cost-drivers" such as their headcount and the number of transactions on their major applications.

The CFO was a strong advocate of allocations. It gave her a better view of the total costs within each business unit. However, Robert paid the price.

Like a slap in the face, these allocations reminded everybody of how expensive IT was. But since they were based on cost-drivers rather than actual consumption of IT products and services, there still wasn't any clear connection to value delivered. Allocations just exacerbated the general perception that IT cost too much.

Robert had hoped that having to pay IT costs would limit clients' demands. But that didn't work. Allocations are not a "pay for what you bought" model (fee for service), where charges directly result from specific purchase decisions. There were cost pools for desktop computers, network services, applications hosting, and so on. But the details were fuzzy. And clients couldn't choose not to buy any of these high-level cost pools.

So clients didn't believe that limiting their demands would materially reduce their allocations.

To make matters worse, since allocations seemed unrelated to clients' purchase decisions, they were viewed as "taxation without representation." Of course, nobody likes being out of control of their costs, especially business-unit executives in this margin-conscious company. Naturally, business leaders attempted to gain back some degree of control. Their bonuses were on the line!

Since they didn't believe they could control costs by limiting their demands, clients attempted to reduce allocations by micro-managing Robert. They challenged Robert's costs at every opportunity.

For example, Robert tried to establish an "account representative" function to improve relationships with the business and better align IT with business strategies. Despite the proven value of such a function, executives refused to pay for it through their allocations.

(Imagine telling any of your vendors that you want them to remove the cost of their sales force from the price they charge you! But that's essentially what business-unit leaders did to Robert.)

By the way, these same executives expected regular account reviews. And they complained that the IT department didn't understand their businesses. They just didn't want to pay for the account representatives who would do exactly that. Sadly, this issue became so politicized that Robert shelved the initiative.

This meddling further strained relations; and it created a political distraction, when the dialog really should have been focused on identifying the best investments in IT's products and services, and opportunities for savings through demand reduction.

Adding to the controversy, everybody felt that the allocations were unfair. (Funny, they all thought they were paying more than their fair share.... Figure the math!?) Executives challenged the formulas, which were logical but crude. Countless valuable hours were lost justifying why costs were apportioned as they were.

Robert tried to improve the calculations, breaking big cost-pools into smaller pools that were allocated with more refined formulas. But this didn't reduce the controversy. In fact, the more detailed the allocation formulas got, the worse the politics got. The granularity implied that clients had control over their purchase decisions when, in fact, they didn't. And the formulas were even more difficult to understand, engendering even more mistrust.

Allocations succeeded at the CFO's objective of assigning IT costs to business units. But all this effort contributed nothing to sound financial decision making; it didn't control costs; and all this controversy sure didn't help Robert's relationships with his peers.

[For solutions, look up "allocations" in the Index.]

"It's your money; do the best you can with it."

After business units submitted their allocations to Robert, the real trouble began.

Once the money was turned over to Robert, clients viewed every-thing as free. Of course, when price is zero, demand approaches infinity. Like the proverbial kid in a candy story, clients wanted everything because they didn't have to pay for anything.

It seemed clients were saying, "Hey, we gave you all that money. Now we get to demand anything we can dream of. We paid for PCs — why are ours three years old? We paid for email — why are we limited in storage capacity? We paid for applications hosting — why can't we increase volumes by 20 percent and implement a never-ending list of enhancements?"

Robert had no basis for telling clients, "That wasn't covered in our budget; we'll need incremental funding." Budget was associated with costs like travel and training; so nobody knew which projects and services were funded by IT's budget, and which weren't.

Absurd as it may seem, the company gave Robert a finite amount of money, and, in trade, expected infinite services.

When he complained, Robert's boss told him, "Look, it's your budget; it's your job to do the best you can with it. *You* make decisions about priorities."

So the kids clamor for everything in the candy store. Daddy says no because he knows the limit of his checkbook and is aware of other competing demands. And of course when Daddy says no, Daddy is the villain.

Being the one to say no made Robert an obstacle — an adversary whom clients had to convince of the merits of their needs. Beyond that, it made Robert appear arrogant, as if he thought he knew what was best for the company.

The fact is, judging clients' ideas in this way is the opposite of customer focus. Robert had unintentionally set a precedent that his managers began to follow. IT staff came to believe that it was their job to control those "unruly users."

As IT managers judged and filtered clients' requests, and as they set their own priorities (often based on who screamed the loudest, or who had the most political clout), relationships with clients deteriorated further.

Frustration with IT grew far worse when clients realized that they had no way to satisfy even really pressing needs. Since Corporate IT had a monopoly on infrastructure, they couldn't go elsewhere. And Robert had no effective mechanism for receiving additional funding for incremental work.

On occasion, he'd take on additional projects and charge business units the direct costs such as contractors. But then he found that the rest of the IT organization didn't have enough time to support these additional project teams. So everything fell behind.

As clients felt trapped and helpless, their resentment grew.

One of the IT managers suggested that Robert request additional budget to satisfy all these requests. But Robert knew that this wouldn't help. Even if his budget were doubled, clients' demands would still exceed IT's resources. And, realistically, there was no way he was going to get more money.

As hard as he tried to make the right decisions, clients blamed Robert when IT didn't have sufficient resources to deliver projects that they saw as critical to their businesses.

[For solutions, look up "demand management" in the Index.]

"You're so bureaucratic."

Robert knew that he wasn't making friends by saying no to clients. He wanted to get out of that villain role.

Naively, Robert thought that a more fact-based prioritization process would be better received. He designed a detailed service-request form that asked clients to justify why they needed IT products and services.

Once clients submitted service-request forms, IT staff provided cost estimates. The combination of benefits and costs produced a "balanced scorecard" for each request. Robert established a set of principles for evaluating requests, using what industry pundits told him was a "best practice."

Robert remembered having dinner with a CIO from another company who actually said out loud that by making it difficult, only clients who really needed something would persevere through the request process; so only the best investments would actually surface! Secretly, Robert hoped that there was some truth in this.

As it turned out, this seemingly rational approach made things worse, not better. From the clients' point of view, this whole process was infuriating. Why did they have to prove their needs to a *support* function to buy anything from them? Why all this onerous paperwork? And why the long waits before they got an answer? External vendors didn't treat them this way!

Naturally, clients felt that IT was bureaucratic.

In a meager attempt to ease this process, Robert put the form online. But all that did was make IT seem even more distant.

This service-request process did succeed at filtering demand. Robert declined many requests, pointing to the principles to defend his decisions. Of course, that just reinforced clients' belief that IT was the obstacle — an adversary, not their business partner.

For those requests which were approved, the process didn't provide clear guidance on priorities. For the most part, it was "first come, first served." In some cases, managers adjusted priorities based on their limited understanding of payoff to the business, or on technical priorities. If the truth were known, behind-closed-doors political processes also came into play.

From the client's perspective, all these processes were opaque and frustrating. They resented being disempowered — unable to control one of their critical factors of production. And as hard as IT staff worked to get projects out the door, clients grew increasingly angry.

[For solutions, look up "bureaucracy" in the Index.]

"You're unreliable and incompetent."

Robert had always preached the importance of being responsive, and his staff took his admonitions to heart. They sincerely wanted to please their customers and serve the business.

But with his demand-management process only marginally successful, his staff were still under a lot of pressure to do the impossible.

Facing demanding clients, staff felt they had to say yes even when they knew they didn't have sufficient resources to deliver on their promises. They made promises they couldn't keep — dates they couldn't make, or a Rolls-Royce for the price of a Chevrolet.

The results were devastating. In the futile attempt to satisfy the unrealistic expectations of the business — far more than they had resources to deliver — Robert's staff tried to do as many projects as possible. As you might imagine, something had to give:

*   They "robbed Peter to pay Paul," stretching timeframes so that everything came in late and they got blamed for being unreliable.

*   They cut corners on quality and took unadvisable risks, and gained a reputation for poor quality.

*   They didn't have time for customer relationship building, so clients grew increasingly disenfranchised.

*   They cut internal support services (overhead) and other critical sustenance activities, making everybody less productive.

*   Infrastructure investments were postponed, so services became less reliable and more costly.

*   Internal process improvements and organizational improvements were not resourced, so productivity fell and costs rose.

*   Their pace of innovation was decimated for lack of training and product research.

*   Managers demanded more of their staff — more hours and more productivity. Robert's organization became an increasingly uncomfortable place to work — a high-pressure assembly line, surrounded by irate customers, with limited career-growth opportunities. Of course, the best people left. The remainder felt burned out and abused, and many became cynical and gave up trying.

These false economies amounted to "eating your seed corn." Maybe these shortcuts allowed IT to get one or two more projects out the door. But despite all their hard work, Robert's staff still couldn't come close to satisfying clients' unbridled demands.

What they *did* do was sacrifice their organization's capability, quality, competitiveness, credibility, and reputation.

[For solutions, look up "delivery, problems with" in the Index.]

"I haven't got time to help on your project team."

Another unfortunate casualty of unbridled demand was teamwork.

Robert's staff were, by nature, friendly, supportive, and worked well together. Nonetheless, teamwork collapsed.

They didn't need team-building. The problem wasn't a lack of desire to help one another, or a lack of trust in others' capabilities.

The root cause of the problem was resources. Even when one group wanted to help another, it was overcommitted and couldn't be counted on to deliver on its promises.

When staff can't trust one another (due to differing priorities and overcommitments, not a lack of personal integrity), they learn to be self-sufficient. "Stovepipes" developed as managers, who had jobs to do, replicated each other's skills so as not to be dependent on one another.

With less teamwork and staff dabbling in others' domains, there was less use of qualified specialists. As a result, costs rose, and quality and reliability diminished further.

[For solutions, look up "teamwork" in the Index.]

"You're not aligned with business strategies."

Every year, corporate executives revised the company's business strategy. Once the plan was published, people throughout the company were expected to align their work with those strategies.

Robert always did more than just distribute the plan. He met with his management team to ensure that everybody really understood each corporate strategy. He even put "contribution to strategy" in their performance objectives.

Why, then, did he repeatedly hear the complaint that IT was not well aligned with strategy?

The answer was pretty obvious: Managers were too busy responding to clients' day-to-day requests to think about new strategic projects. Every year, IT ended up with less money and more "keep the lights on" operational work than before. That left less each year for new projects, and hence less and less opportunity to contribute meaningfully to business strategies.

So Robert pulled together a small team to study corporate strategies and decide how best to serve them.

This team recommended a short list of projects, including a couple of infrastructure projects that could be justified under the strategies, plus a number of applications-development projects that they thought would help clients deliver their business strategies.

Accustomed to defending IT projects in the budget process, Robert sponsored these projects. He declared these to be the IT organization's top priorities, and began rejecting even more clients' requests to free resources for these "strategic" projects.

Clients were upset. But Robert pointed to the strategic plan when he told them that their requests were not as important as the projects that his team had generated. For some reason, this explanation didn't go over very well.

Faced with challenges from business-unit leaders, Robert had to justify the infrastructure projects to the CFO and CEO. He was adamant about the need, and gained their support. He'd won that battle (and his peers on the executive team felt that they had lost).

However, things didn't go so well for the applications projects on that strategic-projects list. Most required CFO approval for the capital involved, and were killed when the business units that were supposed to benefit from them publicly panned them.

IT was able to complete the few projects which were approved. But clients resisted when Robert tried to foist these solutions on them. It didn't matter whether Robert was right about the payoff. They weren't going to incur the risks and costs of changing their business processes to make Robert look like a hero.

Having been the one who sponsored these projects, Robert had to defend his reputation. He pushed harder to get clients to use his solutions. This further strained relations. And despite his efforts, even good investment decisions turned sour when the expected benefits weren't realized for lack of business commitment.

At the next CIO conference, Robert whined to a friend, "They accuse me of not being aligned with strategy, and then shoot me down when I try. There's nothing I can do."

[For solutions, look up "strategy, alignment" in the Index.]

"We need governance (in the form of a steering committee)."

At this point, Robert got serious about demand management. He set up a "governance process" to foist the villain role off on a steering committee of business-unit executives. While convincing his boss, he cited numerous other CIOs who had done this, and labeled executive steering committees as a "best practice."

The committee's job was to set priorities among the major projects competing for IT's limited resources. Robert hoped this would build clients' understanding of the value of IT and align priorities with business needs, as well as filter demand.

It wasn't a bad idea, but "the devil's in the details."

Of course, the committee only oversaw a portion of Robert's budget — just big projects (perhaps 20 to 30 percent of IT's total budget). The other 70 to 80 percent went to "keeping the lights on" — operations and small projects. So executives still didn't understand where the bulk of the IT budget was going. This governance process did little to address the general feeling that IT cost too much and wasn't delivering enough value for the money.

Meanwhile, the demand for those operational services and small projects remained unconstrained by the committee.

Actually, the steering committee didn't do much to constrain demand for the major projects either. It dutifully rank-ordered the projects. But executives on the committee didn't know where to "draw the line." They lacked two key pieces of information: One, they didn't know how much they were authorized to spend. And two, they didn't know what those major projects would cost.

So they went on expecting *all* the projects — in the sequence they'd specified. Now, instead of yelling at Robert individually, the committee gathered all the top executives together to yell at him in unison!

So Robert had his staff calculate the applications-engineering hours required by each project, and told the committee how many hours in total were available. Now, they knew where to draw the line. But new problems emerged.

At this point, expectations were limited by existing development staff. Were there some high-payoff projects that would have warranted bringing in contractors? Probably, but we'll never know. The committee's job was simply to prioritize projects within currently available hours.

And in many cases, indirect supporting functions which were necessary to deploy these projects (and whose hours were not visible to the committee) became a bottleneck. Approved projects routinely came in late.

In the IT industry, Robert had been reading about "portfolio management." But this sure wasn't it.

Portfolio management is supposed to optimize the overall return on a portfolio of investments. But the steering committee didn't know the ROI on proposed projects, and didn't really manage an investment portfolio.

For example, in one case, they chose as their first priority a big project with a very good payoff, calling it "strategic" because of its size. By investing all the available hours in that one big project, they inadvertently passed up a number of small projects that together would have added up to a much higher payoff.

And thanks to the committee, IT was now looking more bureaucratic than ever. The committee demanded request forms that were even more detailed. Clients had to wait for consideration by the committee. And they had little opportunity to defend their requests; they submitted their paperwork and hoped for the best.

Going from bad to worse, it wasn't long before the steering committee began to overstep its bounds....

On some occasions, business leaders offered Robert incremental funding for projects that didn't get past the steering committee. Robert wanted to use their money to hire contractors and get the jobs done. But the steering committee stepped in and blocked those projects, perhaps out of concern for the delays caused by the shared support function. The committee wasn't just prioritizing Robert's budget; it began managing his entire workload.

As a result, business leaders with money to spend were forced to hire their own IT staff or go directly to vendors to get their needs satisfied — sources which are generally more expensive and less effective than a shared-services function. [3]

It got worse. Rather than simply deciding priorities among major projects, the committee began to act like a board of directors. They presumed they had the power to approve Robert's internal decisions and meddle in IT's operations. They demanded that Robert present infrastructure plans, process changes, and even key hiring decisions.

In short, the steering committee did a poor job of managing demand. It made poor investment decisions. And it became a political albatross for Robert.

[For solutions, look up "steering committee" in the Index.]

"Cut X percent."

Late in the year, bad news arrived. The company anticipated a five percent drop in revenues.

As could be expected, the edict came from on high. Everybody had to take an across-the-board cut. It was left to executives like Robert to figure out how to do this.

Robert didn't have any magic up his sleeve. So he tasked his managers with cutting their costs by five percent. The results were disastrous.

Each manager independently decided what not to do within his/her group. As a result, the decisions on which deliverables were postponed had little relationship to business strategies.

Meanwhile, one manager's top-priority project was cut by another manager whose support services were critical to its success. So even deliverables that weren't supposed to be cut were delayed.

Of course, this further impressed managers that they couldn't depend on one another, so teamwork deteriorated even more. Productivity continued its downward slide.

The managers cut back on training and innovation projects. This affected a number of high-profile deliverables that weren't supposed to be cut, but which required new skills and technologies.

Instead of focusing on doing fewer things, this across-the-board cut led to widespread ineffectiveness, undermining the organization's ability to do anything (even important things) well.

In the end, the five percent cut in costs led to a nearly 20 percent decline in results. Clients might have understood the need for a few sacrifices, but this disaster affected virtually every business unit is some critical ways. Executives were livid.

[For solutions, look up "cost cutting" in the Index.]

"We should outsource you."

Over time, clients grew increasingly unhappy with IT's costs and results. They began grumbling about outsourcing. At least that way they'd have control of their costs and their priorities, and they'd be treated with respect.

Eventually the grumbling grew to a groundswell. So the CFO

initiated an outsourcing study, asking if the company could save money by outsourcing all or a major portion of IT.

Why do people think that outsourcing saves money, despite the fact that vendors have to make a profit on the deal? Vendors' sales pitches can be deceiving:

* "We'll give you 50 percent of what you're getting today for 80 percent of the cost. That's a 20 percent cost savings!"

* "We'll do it for 25 percent less. (Just don't ask us about the quality of service.)"

* "We'll give you the base work for 15 percent less than your internal costs (and then charge a huge premium whenever you ask for anything beyond that)."

* "We'll give you everything for 20 percent less than internal costs (this year... with escalation to make the deal very profitable by the end of the contract)."

To preclude such trickery, the CFO hired a well-known consulting firm to perform a benchmarking study. This consultant had a database of other companies' outsourcing costs, divided into what they called "towers." Each tower represented a major area of IT activity, such as computer infrastructure, network services, applications, and PC support.

The consultant sorted Robert's costs into the same towers for the purpose of comparison. The results were not pretty. Analysis showed that the company could save money with outsourcing in almost every tower.

Robert pointed out that his costs could be higher for any number of reasons.... Unlike other companies in the database, Robert's company had many small healthcare clinics scattered throughout the country. They provided critical healthcare services, 7 days a week, 24 hours a day, with no down-time — lives depended on it. They faced unique regulatory requirements. All these differences drove costs up.

Meanwhile, Robert reminded executives that they had refused to invest in updating his infrastructure; so Robert couldn't bring costs down there.

And, of course, there was that "full cost recovery" mandate which inflated Robert's costs with enterprise-good services that were excluded from the outsourcing deals in the consultant's database.

Cashing in a lot of political chips, Robert finally convinced the CFO that the towers approach to benchmarking was unfair. He promised a more granular comparison of internal costs with vendor costs. This bought him some time.

The following year, Robert made an attempt to calculate rates for some of IT's services, which he compared to vendors' rates.

But often, rates were calculated for big bundles of services. For example, the rate for PCs included a lot more than the hardware. Bundled in were costs of the help desk, network connections, and PC repairs. Naturally, clients believed they could buy a PC for a lot less from outside vendors.

In the applications development group, Robert set a rate per hour for an experienced engineer, complete with office space, tools, and management. Clients compared this ready-to-go employee with a contractor who they'd have to house, equip, train, and manage.

Robert priced storage services at the highest level of quality — response time, frequency of backups, and change control. Clients knew they could buy storage from "the cloud" for far less, but they didn't necessarily recognize that external services were at a much lower level of quality.

Robert's finance manager did the best he could in the time allotted, but the cost model underlying the rates was admittedly crude. It was based on simple activity-based costing, cost pools were large, and the calculations were far from transparent.

Robert couldn't be certain that he wasn't making a profit on some products, while undercharging for others. Of course, clients focused on the rates that seemed high, and ignored those that seemed low.

Even if the cost model had been more accurate, Robert was at a disadvantage due to the "full cost recovery" mandate which forced him to put into his rates many things that vendors didn't include in theirs.

The benchmarking exercise was confusing, controversial, and inconclusive. Again, no outsourcing decision was made.

Robert had won another battle; he wasn't forced to outsource any of the IT function. But he'd lost the war. The experience left clients even more critical of Robert's costs, suspicious due to his lack of transparency, and resentful of his defensive attitude.

And from then on, whenever business units had additional money to spend on IT, they went directly to vendors rather than working through Robert.

[For solutions, look up "outsourcing" in the Index.]

"This consolidation process is a fiasco."

Robert faced an interesting challenge when his company acquired another company of almost equal size. Being the more senior of the two CIOs, he was given responsibility for merging the two IT functions.

After spending some time getting to know his counterpart and the other management team, he placed each of their groups under the appropriate senior manager in his organization.

Obviously there were winners and losers. The managers who came from the other company felt disenfranchised and unfairly treated. Most of the good ones left, taking with them critical institutional knowledge. IT began failing to deliver commitments inherited from the other company, many of which Robert didn't even know about.

The damage went deeper than that. Although many of the labels in the boxes on their organization chart seemed familiar to Robert, they did different things. For example, Robert's applications engineers did their own database engineering. But in the acquired IT group, it was done by the infrastructure group. Now, nobody knew where to go for support services, and the confusion resulted in badly engineered systems and delayed projects.

Robert was under pressure to deliver "synergies" in the form of headcount reductions. So he laid people off to achieve the target savings. But his managers had not had time to integrate the two organizations and gain any real synergies. In fact, with all the chaos, both organizations were *less* productive than they'd been prior to the merger.

The math is simple: Less headcount plus lower productivity equals *far* less results. IT became noticeably less reliable in project and service delivery.

To his dismay, Robert found himself being the poster boy for an acquisition gone awry.

[For solutions, look up "consolidations" in the Index.]

The Bottom Line

Every step of the way, poor Robert had followed industry best practices and tried so hard to solve very real problems of resource governance. Finally, he began to understand that so-called "best practices" may be nothing more than the mistakes everyone else had been making.

Traditional resource-governance processes have a cost — both to the enterprise and to the people involved. They are the root cause of much all-to-real pain, and take an organization in a direction exactly the opposite of what most leaders envision — away from customer focus, entrepreneurship, clear accountability, empowerment, and teamwork. They undermine strategic alignment, shareholder value, relationships, and careers.

After years of struggles and disappointments, Robert was finally ready to try a fresh approach.

---

*The conventional view serves to protect us
from the painful job of thinking.*

John Kenneth Galbraith

THE VISION

4. Basic Principles of Internal Market Economics

Imagine someone running for the Presidency of the country on the following platform:

All corporate revenues will be turned over to the government immediately upon receipt.

Legislators will then decide how to distribute the money back to corporations so that they can pay their bills. How will they determine how much each corporation gets? They'll decide what capital infrastructure (plant and equipment) investments each corporation needs, and consider funding some of its major projects. Beyond that, they'll just match last year's spending, plus or minus a percentage based on total federal revenues.

And while the legislature may decide on some major projects, for the most part, corporations will decide for themselves which products and services to make and who gets them.

So the way to get what you need from corporations will be to wait in line, harass the staff of the corporation, lobby with the legislature, or if you're really important, get yourself on the corporation's board of directors.

And we'll measure the success of corporations based on whether they spent what they forecasted (not whether they produced anything for anybody).

"Absurd!" you say. Of course it is.

So why would we believe this can work *within* organizations?

Let's recast this same platform, but this time inside a corporation:

The corporation owns all revenues — money coming from externally facing business units.

The executive leadership team decides how to distribute that money in the form of departmental budgets. They decide on the funding for capital investments proposed by organizations, and consider funding some major projects; beyond that, they just match budgets to last year's spending, plus or minus a percentage based on total forecasted revenues.

And while the executive leadership team decides on a few major projects, for the most part, organizations decide for themselves which products and services to make, and who among their internal customers gets them.

So the way to get what you need from internal service providers is to wait in line, harass the staff of the organization, lobby with top executives, or if you're really important, get yourself on the organization's steering committee.

And we measure the success of organizations based on whether they spend no more than their budgets.

Sound familiar? Absurd as it may be, that's exactly how the "internal economy" works in too many cases.

We all understand the alternative — market economics — on the national level:

Corporations own the revenues they earn.

They use their money to buy supplies — staff, materials, services, and capital — since they know best what they need in order to produce the products and services that their customers wish to buy.

Their vendors make every effort to deliver what they choose to buy, because that's where vendors' revenues come from.

What corporations produce is driven by customers who decide what they buy, based on their deep understanding of their own needs as well as knowledge of how much is in their checkbooks.

And government takes a share of every corporation's profits in the form of taxes to pay for services that are good for society as a whole — things that no single company would (or should) pay for, like defense, safety, roads, and the social safety net which is at the foundation of a stable society.

> (Okay, that part gets controversial. But since we're not here to discuss politics, let's refocus on the economy.)

In summary, everybody buys what they most need, and pays for what they choose to buy.

Thanks to market economics at the national level:

* Resources flow to the most valued products and services — the best investments (whether or not returns are quantified).

* Corporations are automatically aligned with their customers' needs.

* Corporations get the money they need (via revenues) to produce what's expected of them (as long as they price their products and services at or above cost). And they can borrow money (which they have to pay back) for major investments.

* Customers don't expect more than they can afford. Sure, they may wish for more; but their expectations are constrained by their spending power.

*   Teams form globally as companies subcontract for what they need, and subcontractors in turn buy what they need from others, and so on.

*   Corporations take risks and develop new products and services in a creative, entrepreneurial manner.

---

*Market economics is **the** most powerful mechanism of social coordination known to mankind.*

Dr. Ed Lindblom
Professor Emeritus of Economics and Political Science
Yale University

At the heart of market economics is this key principle: <u>Customers control spending power, and decide what they'll buy</u>.

More specifically:

*   Customers know how much money they have to spend.

*   Customers know what products and services are available, and how much they cost.

*   Customers decide what they'll buy.

*   Customers are accountable for the return on their purchase decisions.

*   Customers are accountable for living within their means, and have to come up with more money if they want to buy more.

Meanwhile, successful companies know they have to earn customers' business (striving for the position of vendor of choice) by doing the following:

*   Offer a broad, relevant catalog of products and services.

*   Offer the best value (quality/price).

*   Keep their products and services up to date (through innovation).

*   Deliver on their contracts reliably and with quality.

*   Build excellent relationships with customers.

Markets work in the real world. So let's envision how market economics works *within* organizations.

Transparency is often just as effective as a rigidly applied rule book and is usually more flexible and less expensive to administer.

Gary Hamel
Author [4]

Instead of the traditional bureaucratic view of organizations as hierarchies of control, consider every little group within the enterprise as a small *business within a business.*

Managers are not there just to manage the resources and processes under them, but rather to run little businesses that "sell" products and services (whether or not money changes hands) to customers.

Customers may be other groups within the same department, clients throughout the enterprise, external customers, or the board of directors (for enterprise-good services). Most groups serve combinations of these customers. But everybody must have customers for their products and services.

Clients (business units) may buy products and services individually, or they may come together to form consortia to buy shared products and services. But in either case, internal products and services are never forced on clients. Clients are in control of what they buy from internal service providers.

You're gonna have to serve somebody.

Bob Dylan [5]

Of course, products and services are priced to cover the supplier's costs. So instead of getting a budget to cover their expenses, organizations get revenues for their sales, which cover their costs. (This does not have to mean fee-for-service chargebacks, as is explained in the next chapter.)

In this internal marketplace, customers only buy what's economic. They buy what they need, but not things that cost more than they're worth. Thus, internal service providers are automatically aligned with the business needs and strategies of their customers.

This alignment goes deep into every organization. To satisfy externally facing business units, internal service providers buy what they need from others (within the same organization, and elsewhere in the enterprise). As a result, alignment ripples throughout an entire enterprise — everybody serving their immediate customers and hence ultimately serving the needs of externally facing business units.

This can happen in real time. Data mining of customer calls and web hits produces early indicators of enterprise performance. This data may be gathered by call centers and IT, but it's of primary interest to product managers. If they use this real-time data to adjust what they buy from all their internal suppliers (who, in turn, adjust what they buy to meet their now-revised deliverables), real-time data can ripple through the entire enterprise, keeping everyone aligned with rapidly shifting market conditions.

Individual accountabilities are crystal clear, and results are measured objectively based on whether managers deliver the products and services they promised at a competitive price.

Most managers face plenty of competition in the form of outsourcing and decentralization. But even where internal service providers are granted monopolies or where outsourcing isn't a realistic alternative, price and quality comparisons — benchmarks as part of people's performance appraisals — keep internal entrepreneurs competitive. Thus, managers continually improve their processes and control their costs.

And every customer knows that he/she can't expect more of internal suppliers than he/she can afford. Thus, expectations match resources.

[Internal market economics] addresses all the
major issues that we currently have.
It's completely different from the way we
did things before, but it just makes sense.

Doug Volesky
Assistant Administrator for Enterprise Services
Information Technology Services Division
State of Montana [6]

Chapters 5 through 8 explain how internal resource-governance processes can be designed based on this vision and these principles of market economics.

Note on semantics:

Throughout this book, the word *"enterprise"* will refer to an entire corporation, or a relatively autonomous company (division) within a corporation. In government, it refers to a branch or relatively autonomous agency. An enterprise is generally intended to serve customers in other legal entities.

The word *"organization"* will refer to a department or business unit within an enterprise reporting to a single supervisor, which produces deliverables for others but is not designed to serve customers outside the enterprise without help from other organizations in the enterprise.

An *"internal service provider"* is an organization whose customers are primarily within the enterprise.

"Clients" are people outside your organization.

"Customers" are people who buy your products and services (whether or not money changes hands). They may be clients, or they may be other groups within your organization (your peers).

"Suppliers" are people from whom you buy things, including other groups within your organization, clients, and vendors.

Note that the terms "customer" and "supplier" refer to a relationship, not a group of people.

(Additional definitions of terminology used in this book are provided in the Glossary.)

5. How Money Flows:
Revenues Distinct from Expenses

Let's return to Robert's challenge of managing clients' expect-ations (described in Chapter 3).

Of course, the phrase "managing expectations" doesn't really mean manipulating other people's feelings. It refers to the *processes that cause people to understand what can be expected of an organization for a given level of funding.*

"Demand management" is a closely related concept. It refers to the *processes that filter clients' demands to fit within available resources.*

This chapter describes market-based demand-management processes (with or without chargebacks).

Tragedy of Commons

In traditional financial processes, you're given a budget to pay your expenses. It's yours to spend as you see fit. It's your job to manage your resources in a way that best serves your internal customers. This old paradigm suggests that *you* make decisions about priorities (instead of customers deciding what they'll buy from you).

These traditional financial processes create a classic problem in economics. The "tragedy of commons" refers to any situation where individuals benefit from apparently "free" resources. The vivid example that Garrett Hardin, professor of human ecology, used to illustrate this dynamic is the animal herder who uses a

pasture shared with others (a "commons"). [7] If he expands his
herd, he gains all the benefits; but the cost is shared among all the
herders who use the pasture. His rational course of action is to
expand as much as possible. Since all herders reach the same
conclusion, overgrazing is inevitable.

Robert experienced exactly this. IT was a "commons" to clients,
since everything appeared free. Like kids in a candy store, clients
thought they had the right to demand of Robert anything they
might want. He was expected to deliver virtually infinite services
on a finite budget, and it was his fault when his budget wasn't
sufficient to satisfy all his customers' needs.

The key to solving Robert's "managing expectations" problem is
found in market economics.

In market economics, instead of you deciding your own organization's priorities, customers decide what they'll buy from you.

Two ingredients are necessary to make a market work:

*   A defined checkbook which customers own and manage.

*   Prices for everything the organization sells.

Essentially, market economics gives the kids in the candy store an
allowance, and then lets them buy whatever they want.

Sure, customers always want more. We all want more than we
can afford. But we don't blame the store when we can't afford
everything in it. Clients will come to understand that the
constraint is their spending power, not the internal service
provider's resources.

Will clients make wise choices, even if they aren't candy experts?
Of course they will! After all, business unit executives are not

children. They've risen to leadership ranks because they're trusted to make decisions for their business units. They don't need to be experts in their suppliers' professions. They only need to combine their in-depth knowledge of their own businesses with a "smart buyer's" knowledge of what they need from others.

The Role of Chargebacks

On the surface, it may sound as if internal market economics requires a complex system of intra-company charges. But *charge-backs aren't required to make market economics work within organizations*.

This chapter explains how to create the market effect without chargebacks. But first, let's explore the concept of chargebacks.

The term "chargebacks" refers to any money that flows from clients (other organizations) to internal service providers, to pay the costs of products and services delivered.

Terence Quinlan, an early pioneer in chargebacks in the IT industry and founder of the IT Financial Management Association, said, "Chargeback can be one of the most valuable financial-management initiatives because it initiates many of the disciplines necessary to run internal service providers as businesses, including: contracting and service-level agreements, product/service costing and profitability reporting, billing, benchmarking, capacity planning, and management accountability for cost control. It also provides a basis for investment decision making, corporate transfer pricing, and satisfies some regulatory requirements."

This section examines the purpose of chargebacks, and distinguishes two different types of funds transfers.

Cost Accounting

A narrow view of the purpose of chargebacks is to distribute an internal service provider's costs to the business units that consume its support services. Chargebacks are touted as a way to hold business units accountable for all their costs, and to more accurately view business units' contributions to corporate profits.

From this cost-accounting perspective, a chargeback system is working well if it distributes costs fairly — that is, when charges are roughly associated with utilization and key cost-drivers.

As Robert discovered, having this purpose in mind leads to a number of serious problems. Here are just two common consequences:

Problem 1: In pursuit of accuracy, chargeback designers focus on technical cost-drivers and come up with chargeable items that bewilder clients. As a result, clients resent having to pay for things they don't understand. And when they don't understand the complex formulas that went into determining the amounts, clients become suspicious that they're being overcharged.

Problem 2: In search of simplicity, chargebacks bundle a large number of discrete deliverables into a single charge (a "cost pool"). Clients can't turn down the whole bundle; it includes things that they need. So clients rightfully feel that they're being held hostage and have to pay for things they don't want.

Both problems create a situation where clients can't control the charges that hit their bottom lines. Cost accounting creates controversy, and does nothing to support economic decision making.

Demand Management

Another view of the purpose of chargebacks is demand management. If clients' demands have a price attached, they'll think twice about requesting support services.

This is closer to the truth. When there's money at stake, only good investments will be approved.

But just scaring business away can't be the objective.

Internal market economics explains the real purpose of chargebacks: *Chargebacks are prices for specific products and services. They empower clients to control their costs by deciding what they buy from internal service providers. And, of course, chargebacks ensure that internal service providers have the funding they need to satisfy all customers' purchases.*

This definition puts chargebacks in the context of market economics.

Allocations Versus Fee-for-service

Chargebacks take two forms:

*   **Allocations** transfer money from business units to internal service providers in large lump sums, to pay the costs of multiple distinct products and services. Transfers occur periodically (annually, quarterly, or monthly). Amounts are based on high-level "drivers" such as clients' headcount, budget, or a count of some representative transactions.

*   **Fee-for-service** chargebacks transfer money based on specific purchase decisions. Payments are made as products and

services are delivered (typically monthly). Amounts are based on rates for the specific products and services which clients bought.

While it's the most advanced form of internal market economics, fee-for-service isn't right for everyone. There are risks inherent in the premature implementation of fee-for-service chargebacks.

First and foremost, the money truly belongs to clients and they can choose to spend it elsewhere — on decentralization, outsourcing, or something other than your function. This has the advantage of allowing money to freely flow to other purposes or other providers if they offer better returns.

But from the viewpoint of an internal service provider, you face risks. If you are not yet appreciated as their vendor of choice, or if the value of your products and services is not well understood, premature implementation of fee-for-service can lead to a dramatic downsizing of your organization for the wrong reasons.

Another risk is that without the context of market economics — without a catalog with rates set at full cost, and governance processes that guide clients to make sound purchase decisions — fee-for-service chargebacks become an expensive, bureaucratic nightmare that may add little value.

Fee-for-service chargebacks represents the end of an evolutionary spectrum — the purest form of internal market economics. But it's generally not the best first step.

And again, you can gain most of the benefits of internal market economics without fee-for-service chargebacks. Here's how....

Revenues, Not "Cost Recovery"

The first step in understanding internal market economics (with or without chargebacks) is to realize that *you don't get money to cover your costs.* Budgeting is *not* a matter of forecasting and justifying costs, and then perhaps spreading your costs among customers through chargebacks (as in cost accounting).

Instead, as a business-within-a-business, you get *revenues from the sale of products and services* to customers. These revenues pay your costs.

Revenues flow to you from any combination of three sources:

* Direct budget (funding from above).
* Allocations — lump sums to cover multiple purchases.
* Fee-for-service — payments for individual purchases.

With fee-for-service, it's easy to see how market economics works inside enterprises. Clients already control a "checkbook" of funds and decide what they buy from internal service providers.

But for those who aren't ready for fee-for-service, the next step in understanding internal market economics is to think about direct budgets and allocations in a different way.

Budget Revenues

With internal market economics, your budget is not given to you to cover your costs. It's a source of *revenues* to buy your products and services.

Your budget is treated as a *prepaid account* — money put on deposit with you at the beginning of each year in order to buy your products and services throughout the year ahead.

To illustrate this concept, consider the "level payment plans" offered by utilities such as my fuel-oil supplier. I'd like to avoid a $2000 bill when they fill my tank with oil at the beginning of the heating season. So my supplier allows me to pay a few hundred dollars a month throughout the year.

It's not that they're promising all the oil I might need for the fixed price of a few hundred dollars per month. During the summer, I build up a positive balance in my prepaid account. Then, when they deliver that tank of oil, they bill me at market rates. I pay them, using the money already on deposit in my prepaid account.

The prepaid account is my money, until I spend it on oil. If I change oil suppliers, they have to give it back to me. Of course, if I buy more oil than is afforded by that prepaid account, I have to give them more money.

Similarly, your direct budget is a prepaid account that belongs to your clients. It pays for the multitude of products and services that they buy from you. And if they want more than it pays for, they need to come up with more money.

Figure 1 shows the flow of revenues in an internal market economy.

When you receive your annual budget, you separate out budget for investments in your organization such as infrastructure and major improvements, and for enterprise-good activities like policy coordination. That portion of your budget is yours to manage.

(These set-asides, termed "Subsidies" and "Ventures," are defined in Chapter 8.)

Figure 1: Money Flows

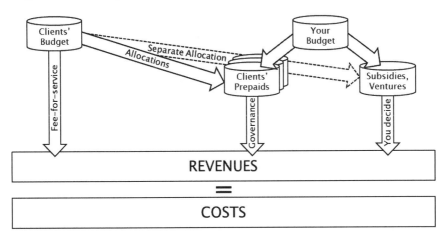

This leaves the bulk of your budget for client deliverables. This portion of your budget flows into a "checkbook" that exists within your accounts but belongs to clients. In Figure 1, it's labeled "Clients' Prepaids."

Then, clients decide which of your products and services to buy throughout the year, paying for their purchases with this prepaid account. In Figure 1, this check-writing decision process is labeled "Governance."

By treating your budget as a pre-paid account and giving client control of that checkbook, the market effect can be implemented without actual chargebacks.

Allocations

Allocations can be treated in the same way — as a prepaid account. But since the prepaids are submitted by each business unit (rather than from above), they're put in separate checkbooks owned by each business unit. Each business unit then gets to decide which products and services it buys with that money.

This is quite different from the common view of taxing clients to pay your costs, or a fixed price for a big bundle of products and services which they have to buy all at once. Allocations are a way for clients to put money on deposit with you in order to pay for the many distinct products and services they choose to buy.

By turning control of allocations back to clients, a normally contentious and unconstructive process can be turned into something useful to both internal service providers and clients.

Typically, allocations are used to pay for the basic "keep the lights on" services which can be reliably planned. Discretionary projects and additional services are then funded on a fee-for-service basis.

But there's no reason why clients can't freely set the level of their allocations. If they decide on an allocation that's too small, they may have to find additional funding later in the year to pay for all the products and services they need.

What value do allocations offer? They give both clients and internal service providers a degree of predictability.

Stick to the Plan

Typically, budgets are planned well in advance of the start of the fiscal year. Of course, nobody is clairvoyant. The world is constantly changing. Economic conditions change; competitors make moves; technologies evolve; laws and regulations shift; threats appear; opportunities come and go.

Given this volatility, business strategy is certainly not "long term." Some strategies extend over years, while others may have a life-span of months or weeks.

It's foolish to believe that executives can decide exactly which projects and services will be needed a year in advance. A volatile world means that the list of deliverables approved during the budget process, or during any planning process, drifts out of alignment with the needs of the enterprise over time.

It may be tempting to ask clients to commit to the projects and services they agreed to in the planning process, to protect internal service providers from the risk of reduced revenues which don't cover costs. But this would distort the market. Making clients buy things they no longer want may force them to pay for poor investments, and forego better returns elsewhere.

It's generally better to accept an explainable negative variance (a loss) at year end.

There is an exception: If an internal supplier makes a multi-year commitment to an external expense (such as a big asset to be depreciated, or a long-term vendor contract) for a specific customer (or small set of customers), then a multi-year contract with internal customers is warranted.

Similarly, if volumes grow dramatically, suppliers may have to use more staff-augmentation contractors or vendor services (at a higher cost) than was anticipated, causing a loss at the promised rate. Limiting demand would only send internal customers to alternative suppliers (decentralization or outsourcing), which may be more expensive. It's not wise for an entrepreneur to encourage clients to buy elsewhere.

Again, an explainable negative variance is a better alternative, with a mid-year rate adjustment only in the most extreme situations.

(Both of these risks can be mitigated to a great extent by a good cost model, as described in Appendix 3.)

Contrary to an expectation that the business will stick to the plan, clients should have the freedom to adjust what they buy throughout the year.

Budgeting Versus Purchase Decisions

Internal market economics empowers clients to continually adjust priorities throughout the year.

How does this work?

An annual planning process allocates the enterprise's scarce resources into budgets. Essentially, it fills up checkbooks based on the investment opportunities known at that point in time.

Then, throughout the year, "pursers" decide what checks to write based on business conditions at the time.

When things change, such as crises, evolving strategies, or new opportunities, pursers adjust what they buy from internal service providers. This purchase-decision process is sometimes called "governance" or "portfolio management."

The effectiveness of the purchase-decision process determines how well aligned an internal service provider is with its clients' ever-changing business needs and strategies.

The Role of Pursers

Both direct budgets and allocations create checkbooks owned by clients, sitting in the accounts of an internal service provider. Who is the "purser" who controls these checkbooks and decides what checks to write?

The purser for a checkbook should fairly represent the internal clients who benefit from the funding.

In the case of direct budget, it may be a committee representing the entire enterprise, or the checkbook may be divided among the business units and managed independently by each.

In the case of allocations, each business unit funds its own check-book and appoints its own purser.

Where a special budget is designated for an enterprisewide purpose (such as ERP in IT), the purser may be a consortium of clients.

The purser may be a committee, but it's not a "steering committee" with an open-ended charter to "govern" you. There are number of things that a purser committee should *not* do:

*   It should not serve as a "board of directors" overseeing your entire function. Doing so is a conflict of interests, since clients' interests may be short term and parochial, while a board of directors looks after the long-term well-being of the

business it helps to manage. A separate committee may be
needed (albeit with many of the same members) if your boss
feels the need for help managing you.

*   It should not review projects funded directly by business units.
    Business units have a right to buy whatever they wish on a
    fee-for-service basis without committee approval. And since
    your products and services are priced at full cost (including all
    the necessary support services), these additional sales do not
    impinge on pursers' checkbooks or your ability to deliver all
    they purchased.

*   It should not be the decision-maker for the portion of your
    budget intended for internal investments in your infrastructure
    and processes, nor for enterprise-good activities.

The purser committee has a well-defined purpose: to write checks
from the checkbook created by your direct budget or allocations.
That's it.

Pursers should be given purview over the entire client-benefitting
part of your budget (and allocations), not just major projects.

A large portion of each checkbook may be spent at the beginning
of the year on annual service agreements for the "keep the lights
on" deliverables. These decisions may be obvious, but it's still
worthwhile to engage clients. At a minimum, it builds their
understanding of the value you deliver, and why your organization
costs what it does. Beyond that, it gives clients an incentive to
shut down less-valuable services to free resources for new things.
Maybe they'll turn some lights off.

Once annual service agreements are decided, the remaining portion
is available for discretionary projects.

Spending Approval Process

Of course, pursers have to live within their means. All your products and services have a cost. When pursers' checkbooks run out, you stop work.

As an internal service provider, your job is to deliver anything that's funded — and no more. Clients can't expect you to deliver more than they can afford. And you don't have the resources to do more.

Pursers decide what checks to write throughout the year. As new business needs arise during the year, clients make a case to their pursers who decide whether or not to fund the proposal.

If there's not enough money in pursers' checkbooks to fulfill pressing needs, it's the pursers' job to either adjust priorities within the limits of their existing checkbooks, or supply more money. They may forego marginal (albeit planned) deliverables in order to fund newly discovered high-payoff opportunities. They may cut back on the scope of projects to make them more affordable. Or they may supply more money by defending a budget increase for you, or by increasing their allocations.

That failing, clients can find other sources of funding and pay you directly (fee for service). As long as they're willing to pay full cost, you can expand your capacity (e.g., with contractors and vendors) and satisfy the incremental demand. (Internal service providers are not resource constrained, as discussed in Chapter 9.) This way, there's no need to miss good investments or postpone them until the next fiscal year.

This check-writing process deals with new projects, changes in the scope of existing projects, new services, and changes in service levels. It also handles the problem of "scope creep" by ensuring that any material changes in project scope are explicitly funded (or postponed).

Many Small Requests

If executives on the purser committee don't want to be bothered approving many small requests, there are two options:

*   They may set aside a portion of their checkbook for small requests (creating a sub-checkbook), and define who gets to benefit from it and what products and services are eligible for those funds (entitlements).

    Then, requests which meet those criteria are automatically approved, and funded from that sub-checkbook.

    (This is described in Chapter 23, under "Components" in the sub-section titled "Automated Order Entry (Request Management).")

*   They may assume first-in/first-out, or delegate to a sub-committee the initial prioritization. Then, each executive on the purser committee may ask a subordinate to review the prioritized request list and point out any specific items that deserve discussion at the next purser committee meeting (projects that may warrant a higher priority).

But even if they take these shortcuts, pursers remain responsible for the returns on their entire investment portfolios.

Checkbook Accounting and Invoicing

By treating direct budgets and allocations as prepaid accounts under the control of client-appointed pursers, you gain most of the benefits of fee-for-service chargebacks without the risks or costs. However, it does require a bit of incremental accounting.

For both direct budgets and allocations (all the prepaids), the checkbooks exists within the accounts of the internal service provider. Checkbook balances must be maintained.

Invoices must be issued for the products and services actually delivered, just like for fee-for-service chargebacks. Invoices decrement checkbooks. This way, at any point in time, pursers are aware of how much spending power they have left.

Mock Invoices (Show-backs)

These are not mock invoices (sometimes termed "show-backs"). Mock invoices may help clients spot products and services they can do without. But they're not an effective approach to demand management and governance for a number of reasons:

*   They present only past deliverables; they don't show what's about to be spent in the future.

*   They don't give clients the option to shift spending from lower-payoff deliverables to new, high-payoff projects and services.

*   They don't force clients to make tough choices within the limits of a known checkbook, so there's not a lot of incentive to limit demand.

*   And one of the greatest dangers, they imply that clients can
     control their costs without having yet designed a governance
     process that empowers them to make purchase decisions.

The problem is, mock invoices aren't linked to checkbooks and a
purser-driven check-writing process. They may help clients' see
the value they've received, build trust through transparency, and
illuminate current costs. But all these same benefits, and more,
can be gained through internal market economics — and without
the risks.

So if you're going to invest in an invoicing system, make it pay
off by imbedding it in an internal market economy.

6. How Budget Planning Works: Investment-based Budgeting

There are two key prerequisites to internal market economics: pursers need to know how much money is in their checkbooks, and how much things cost.

This chapter examines the process by which checkbooks are filled — budgeting. The next chapter explains how rates for products and services are calculated.

What Is a Budget?

A budget is a source of funding. It fills up a checkbook, which pursers can then spend.

("Budget" is not to be confused with a spending cap imposed on internal service providers which are funded through chargebacks. Budget is money that can pay the bills; spending caps cannot. Spending caps are discussed in Chapter 9.)

If you receive most of your revenues in the form of a direct budget, budgeting means gaining funding for all the products and services your clients will buy.

If you get your revenues from clients (fee-for-service chargebacks or allocations), there are two sections to a budget:

* Most of your budget is an advisory to clients, to help them get enough money in their budgets to buy what they need from you.

* A smaller portion of your budget may bring funding directly

to you for enterprise-good services and for your own infrastructure and business-improvement projects. Counter to the notion of "full cost recovery," these things should always be funded by direct budget, not by clients. (See Chapter 8.)

In most organizations, budgets result from an annual planning process.

Even in organizations that update budgets during the year ("rolling budgets") or continually, annual planning helps an organization anticipate resource requirements and prepare its productive capacity; it helps an enterprise anticipate its cash and capital requirements; and it helps everybody make decisions that have long lead times.

The Challenge of Budget Decision-making

Executives have a sense of how much money (operating expense and capital) will be available in the coming year. In an enterprise budget process, their job is to allocate that money to business units and support functions.

Of course, everybody wants more money. The total of the requests coming from these various organizations always exceeds available funds. The challenge is to allocate scarce resources in a way that will optimize shareholder value (or, for government and not-for-profit enterprises, their missions).

Setting budgets based on current headcount and expenses may not accomplish this objective. Past budgets may have funded low-payoff activities in some areas, and missed great investment opportunities in others. And the future may not be just like the past.

Ideally, organizations' budget should be decided based on the needs of the business and the investment opportunities available in the coming year, i.e., based on returns on investments and strategic relevance.

Deliverable by deliverable, executives should allocate money to the best investment across the entire enterprise, then the next best, and then the next after that, until available funds are committed (technically, until the rate of return on the next best investment drops below the weighted-average, risk-adjusted cost of capital). In simple terms, fund all good investments, and no more.

The entire budget should be zero-based, including "keep the lights on" services. Obviously, keeping the enterprise running is a great investment. But there may be some operational services that should be discontinued to free funds for new, high-payoff initiatives, or to lower costs.

Investment-based Budgeting

To allocate budgets this way, executives must understand the returns on investments in each organization's proposed projects and services. They may not need to quantify everything, but they need a sense of what they'll get for a given level of funding.

Note that when you go to the grocery store, the manager doesn't ask you to pay a share of his rent, electricity, check-out clerks, etc. His "funding request" is based on the price of grocery products.

The same is true within an enterprise. In an internal market economy, a *budget describes the cost of the products (projects) and services you propose to deliver* — your outputs, not your inputs — what you propose to "sell," not just what you want to spend.

This is termed "investment-based budgeting." [8]

Picture a spreadsheet, where the columns represent expense-codes such as salaries, travel and training expenses, licenses and vendor services, etc. The rows represent deliverables — specific products (projects) and services for specific clients. (See Figure 2.)

This kind of spreadsheet is a common, and a sensible, way to develop a budget.

Figure 2: Budget Spreadsheet

EXPENSE CODES

DELIVERABLES	Compensation	Travel	Training	Licenses	
Client Project 1	$	$	$	$	$
Client Project 2	$	$	$	$	$
Client Service 1	$	$	$	$	$
Client Service 2	$	$	$	$	$
Enterprise-good 1	$	$	$	$	$
Venture Project 1	$	$	$	$	$
	$	$	$	$	$

The mistake many organizations make this: After filling in the cells in the spreadsheet, most organizations total the columns instead of the rows, and present a budget for each of the expense-codes. In other words, their budget is an estimate of how much money each manager wants to spend on various costs such as compensation, travel, training, and so on.

The crux of the problem is that this traditional budget doesn't give executives an understanding of what they're buying — what specific products and services they can expect to receive.

An investment-based budget totals the rows, applying all costs to the deliverables planned for the coming year. This is fundamental to portfolio management. It provides the list of investment opportunities and their estimated costs.

Of course, with a transparent cost model underlying an investment-based budget, executives can examine the columns. But their job is to decide what they'll buy, not tell you how to run your business. (Chapter 9 explains why haggling over expenses during the budget process is not an effective or appropriate means of cost control.)

A proposed budget includes not just what you think the enterprise can afford, but also all the requests that clients have made and all the creative ideas that you'd like them to consider. This way, you don't take it upon yourself to decide which of your clients' ideas are worthwhile and which are not; you avoid being an obstacle. And you may be pleased to see that a few new projects and services are approved, granting you a budget beyond your expectations.

On the down-side, if clients don't buy as much as you'd hoped, you may have to shrink your organization. But in practice, this is rare. And even if this happens, it's far better to run a smaller, sane business than to suffer Robert's fate.

Chapter 22 explains how to create an investment-based budget.

Note for U.S. Federal government organizations: Investment-based budgeting satisfies OMB-300 on "Program-based Budgeting," which requires analysis of, and budgeting based on, the total cost (organizationwide) of projects and services. Others may refer to this same concept as "performance-based budgeting."

Filling Checkbooks

Once an investment-based budget is decided, the money flows into checkbooks.

For direct budgets, it's clear how much is slated for enterprise-good services and for investments in your infrastructure and processes. These are specific rows in the budget. These funds go into a checkbook that you manage. The rest goes into a checkbook controlled by client pursers.

For allocations, the client portion of your budget is given to business units. Then, it's returned to you through allocations and placed in client-owned checkbooks. The total cost of the rows sold to each business unit provides a good basis for setting allocation amounts.

And with fee-for-service chargebacks, the client portion of your budget is simply given to business units to spend as they see fit.

7. How Prices are Set

Knowing how much is in the checkbooks is one prerequisite to internal market economics; the other is knowing how much your products and services cost.

Costs are linked to products and services in two ways:

*   An investment-based budget forecasts the *total* cost of proposed products and services (as described in Chapter 6).

*   Rates are *unit* costs, such as the cost per billable hour for labor.

This chapter delves into how costs are assigned to an organization's products and services for both these purposes. It explains why full-cost is preferable to market-based or direct-cost-only rates; the treatment of outsourcing costs; and the importance of accuracy.

The Value of Rates

You set rates, whether you know it or not. Even if you don't publish a price list, you establish an implicit rate when you promise a certain level of service for a given budget.

In an internal market economy, rates are explicit — published in a catalog of products and services.

Obviously, rates are essential for internal service providers that charge fee-for-service for any portion of their sales.

But rates are relevant to all organizations, with or without charge-backs, for the following purposes:

*   Rates are needed to issue invoices as work is delivered, so that pursers know how much they have left to spend.

*   Rates are used to estimate the cost of incremental work that arises mid-year.

*   Rates send signals to customers about the opportunity cost to the enterprise of their purchase decisions. With this informa-tion, customers can decide whether or not it's economic to buy a product or service.

*   Rates provide the best basis for competitive benchmarking (outsourcing comparisons). (See Chapter 13.)

Market-based Pricing

When an internal service provider produces deliverables at cost (presumably less than what vendors would charge), it's generating a profit for the enterprise. It's just that this profit appears on its clients' books, not its own. Clients profit because they're acquiring products and services at below-market rates.

Some have proposed that internal service providers charge at market-based rates rather than at cost. This would make them for-profit businesses within a business (profit centers).

Even when internal service providers are run as profit centers, generally they can charge below-market rates, since their sales and marketing costs are lower. Doing so shares the benefit of this insider advantage with the rest of the enterprise.

There are problems with market-based pricing. The notion of an internal service provider earning a profit is offensive to some and politically delicate. It may make internal service provider seem arm's length, and not really "part of the family." And it may inappropriately encourage decentralization, where business units feel they can fulfill their needs themselves without a mark-up (ignoring the fact that they, too, should be meeting return-on-assets targets).

Nonetheless, there are advantages to this most-advanced stage of internal market economics.

For one, without profits, internal service providers cannot promise projects at a fixed fee. If there were to be an overrun, the internal service provider must still break even. So the overrun is either charged to the enterprise, that is, to all clients, which is grossly unfair; or, the overrun is charged to the specific client of that project, which is no longer fixed-fee.

But if an internal service provider is allowed to earn a profit, it can absorb the costs of overruns (reduce its profits, or risk a loss) if necessary. Thus, fixed-fee contracts are feasible.

A profit center also has more flexibility in pricing. It can price certain products as loss-leaders, combating external vendors that are trying to "buy the business." It can also better compete with external competitors by providing volume discounts.

Market-based pricing also improves the metrics of internal service providers. Return-on-assets becomes a relevant metric of whether an internal service provider is contributing to shareholder value, a metric not available to a breakeven business.

Furthermore, pricing at market rates improves the economic validity of purchase decisions. Cost-based rates may include the cost of capital, but they don't incorporate the enterprise's required returns on assets employed by internal service providers (over and above the cost of capital). Without such profit targets built into rates, clients may buy more than is economic.

Despite these advantages, few internal service providers are run as profit centers. The benefits just aren't worth the political costs. For internal service providers, rates are generally set to equal costs (as not-for-profit businesses within a business).

Of course, pricing can be market- rather than cost-based for products and services sold outside the enterprise.

By the way, even in business units which only sell externally at market rates, analysis of the full costs of their products and services is beneficial. It's the basis for product-line profitability analysis. [9]

Direct (Marginal) Cost Pricing

On the other extreme, some have suggested that internal service providers charge clients only for the direct (marginal) costs of their purchases, and fund fixed (indirect) costs through allocations or via the direct budget. They believe this is simpler (it is), and that it will more accurately recover indirect costs (it will).

They also argue that it will prevent customers from cancelling contracts for infrastructure that the enterprise cannot shed quickly. For example, in IT, a mass exodus from an old mainframe computer leaves IT with an unfunded albatross.

> (This problem could be solved just as well by establishing long-term service contracts with clients whenever an internal service provider must make long-term commitments to depreciate assets or to vendor contracts.)

Although it has some benefits, direct-cost pricing leads to a number of very serious problems:

*   Direct-cost pricing sends inappropriate price signals to the internal marketplace. By implying that products and services are much cheaper than they really are, it induces customers to buy more than is economic.

*   Allocations of indirect costs create all kinds of problems (as Robert experienced). They confront clients with costs unrelated to value. Clients resist paying for indirect costs that are outside their control (remember, "taxation without representation"). This induces inappropriate meddling in how internal service providers run their organizations. And allocations engender resentment and mistrust.

    Note that allocations which are purely indirect costs cannot be treated as prepaids (as described in Chapter 5).

*   The organization finds it difficult to expand support services and infrastructure as its business grows, since increasing the indirect-cost allocation is always controversial.

    This creates bottlenecks, and forces the primary delivery staff to do work that could be done by less-expensive or more-specialized support staff. As the business grows and support staff are stretched more thinly, the result is higher total costs, lower quality, and delays.

*   Like support services, ongoing investments in the organization's capabilities (which are, by nature, indirect) are difficult to expand as the business grows.

    Imagine a software company that prices its products at the cost of a CD and a box. Or a car manufacturer that prices vehicles at the cost of parts and labor. There would be no money available for the development of future products, for sales and marketing, even for managing the firm.

Even costs as fundamental as professional development and process improvements are in jeopardy. They must be debated as budget items since they're not imbedded in rates; and corporate executives are often quite willing to cut them. As a result, providers become less and less efficient over time.

*   Direct costs cannot be compared to competitive benchmarks. This covers lots of sins. An internal service provider can be very inefficient and still appear cheaper than external vendors who must recover indirect costs in their prices.

*   Clients may avoid doing business with the organization, even when it is the best value, because they don't want to trigger an increase in their allocations or get hit with hidden charges via allocations.

For example, in a large diversified company, a divisional IT executive refused to *ever* buy the testing service offered by Corporate IT. She feared that if she used the service at all, Corporate IT would hire staff to fulfill her occasional needs. Then, if these people sat idle between her requests, they would drive up her allocation. The CIO assured her that they wouldn't build excess capacity; they'd staff to the valleys and bring in contractors to handle peak loads. Nonetheless, she didn't want to be at the mercy of his staffing decisions. To her, costs seemed more controllable (albeit higher) if she used vendors rather than Corporate IT.

Marginal (direct) costs should be used to make decisions on the margin. For example, when considering an investment to improve an internal process, it's correct to look only at what changes as a result of that decision. This is why "lean accounting" makes sense; its purpose is to analyze process improvements, and hence it only looks at what actually changes when a process is changed (not at indirect costs which may not change).

However, direct costs do not represent the true long-term cost of providing products and services. As all accountants know, nothing is fixed in the long term. The concept of "fixed" costs only refers to those costs which change in steps rather than continuously, or those which take time to adjust. So expanding direct costs ultimately will expand indirect costs as well.

For example, a facilities department has a building that has unoccupied space in it. A business unit (a tenant of that building) is hiring a new employee as part of a business initiative. Is adding one more office free because the space is available? And does the next business initiative after that, which triggers the need for an additional building, have to pay for the entire cost of that new building? Does the ROI of these two business initiatives change based on the order in which they're considered?

In IT, the same questions arise when a new application fills the remaining capacity on a server, and the next application after that triggers the purchase of a new server.

Obviously, the "straw that breaks the camel's back" should not be burdened with the entire cost of new fixed assets; every user of an asset should bear part of the total cost of the asset.

Thus, even when costs rise in a step function (e.g., where capacity is bought in chunks), each customer should pay a fair share of the total cost — and that's exactly what "full cost" means.

Full-cost Pricing

With internal market economics, you charge customers only for
what they choose to buy (and never charge them for anything they
don't buy and can't control). Therefore, indirect costs (e.g.,
general and administrative costs) are not funded directly, as line
items in your budget.

To do this, rates must include a fair share of all indirect costs.
That is, customers pay the *full cost* to shareholders/taxpayers/
donors of the products and services they buy.

This way, whenever internal entrepreneurs are funded to deliver a
product or service, some portion of the revenues goes to covering
the costs of all the necessary support services and sustenance tasks
which clients don't see.

Peter F. Drucker stressed the importance of full cost (which he
called "activity-based costing") to management decision making:

"Traditional cost accounting measures what it costs to do a task,
for example, to cut a screw thread. Activity-based costing [full
cost] also records the cost of not doing, such as the cost of
machine downtime, the cost of waiting for a needed part or tool,
the cost of inventory waiting to be shipped, and the cost of
reworking or scrapping a defective part. The costs of not doing,
which traditional cost accounting cannot and does not record, often
equal and sometimes even exceed the costs of doing. Activity-
based costing therefore gives not only much better cost control, but
increasingly, it also gives result control." [10]

Of course, indirect costs are subject to executive review. But once
they're scrutinized by an organization's executive and chain of

command, they're not subject to debate by clients. They're built into the rates for the products and services that clients buy.

A "cost model" apportions all indirect costs to the products and services an organization sells. (Cost models are described in Appendix 3.)

Importance of Accuracy

Applying indirect costs to the right products and services is essential. If indirect costs are not correctly apportioned, then some products and services will be overpriced, and others will be underpriced. While the net may be right, distortions in the costs of specific products and services create serious problems.

For products and services which are *overpriced,* the risks include the following:

* Executives may decline good investments because they appear more expensive than they really are.

* Business units may be misled to favor outsourcing or decentralization. If they stop buying overpriced items, the internal service provider will be left with only products and services that are losing money.

* If enterprise-good services are mixed into rates, internal service providers appear to be more expensive than external vendors who don't have to do those things. Then, if clients turn to outsourcing as a result, enterprise-good services will not be funded and the organization will fail to deliver them.

For products and services which are *underpriced,* the risks include
the following:

*   Executives may approve poor investments (or buy too much)
    because they appear less expensive than they really are.

*   As demand for the underpriced items grows, profits from
    overpriced items won't be sufficient to subsidize the losses
    from the sale of underpriced items. Ultimately, the organiza-
    tion will stumble on delivery.

Distortions may ripple through an enterprise. Once an internal
service provider is priced inaccurately, all its customers cannot
price their products and services accurately. Even external pricing
may be inappropriately influenced.

The effects of inaccurate rates ripple through to the balance sheet.
Assets may be inaccurately valued. Inventories may be inaccurately costed.

Given the above risks, it's not appropriate to use rates to
manipulate customers' purchase decisions. Rates based on full
costs will lead customers to make optimal economic decisions.

For example, an IT department may wish to retire an old
mainframe. But it's not right to inflate the rates for mainframe
services to incent clients to transfer their applications to other
platforms. The cost of mainframe computing will go up over
time, and at some point it will be economic for clients to pay the
one-time costs of moving their applications to less expensive
platforms; but until then, moving those applications would not be a
wise investment. Even when that time comes, clients may have

better uses for precious discretionary funds, and may choose to pay somewhat higher rates for a while. Let the market work!

Similarly, it's not appropriate to increase some rates and decrease others to help poor clients who can't afford all they need (and overcharge other clients). An enterprise may decide to use profits from one business unit (the "cash cow") to fund investments in another (a "growth star"). But such decisions are made at the executive level. If executives have chosen not to invest in a business unit, it's not right for internal service providers to circumvent that decision by manipulating their rates.

Both budgeting and rates require an accurate, transparent cost model. With it, you can be confident that your rates are fair, defensible, sustainable, and directly comparable to benchmarks like outsourcing. (See Appendix 3.)

A simple form of cost model — activity-based costing — introduces significant distortions in rates. Appendix 4 discusses second-generation cost models, essential to accurate rates.

Of course, even with a second-generation cost model, there's no such thing as perfect accuracy. When planning future costs, estimates are required. And apportioning indirect costs across multiple rates requires estimates.

However, with a well-structured cost model and planning process, management judgment is structured. Estimates are made of specific assumptions — future spending, proportions, and volumes — not of rates themselves. This greatly improves accuracy.

Accurate rates are especially important to government organizations, and to those funded by them. [11]

8. How Enterprise Costs Are Funded: Subsidies and Ventures

There are two things which are not decided by your clients, and which should not be imbedded in your rates. Contrary to "full cost recovery," these two things should always be funded by direct budgets, even if all client sales are funded through chargebacks.

Subsidies

"Subsidies" are enterprise-good services that an internal service provider does for the *benefit of the enterprise as a whole,* not for individual business units nor for the benefit of your own organization. Unlike overhead, these are things which *competitors (like vendors and decentralized counterparts) don't have to do* (unless they're paid to deliver these distinct services).

Examples include coordination of enterprise policies and standards; enterprise-reputation activities such as public relations; enterprise-safety services; community-action initiatives; coordination of decentralized functional counterparts (e.g., a corporate CFO coordinating business-unit finance groups); and corporate committees which are outside the organization's normal product line.

Here's an example that illustrates the problem of full cost recovery where enterprise-good services are mistakenly imbedded in rates:

Most corporate IT departments research the various brands of personal computers and recommend safe, standard configurations to the enterprise. This is akin to a "consumer-report" function for PCs, reducing costs through standardization and protecting the enterprise from bad products.

If the cost of this research were embedded in the IT department's price per PC, then PCs provided by the IT department would appear unrealistically expensive compared to external sources of exactly the same configurations.

If some clients save money by buying PCs directly from vendors (or establish their own IT departments), research costs would have to be spread into a smaller base. IT's rates would be distorted upward even more, perhaps chasing more business away.

Of course, if everybody bought their PCs elsewhere, there would be no funding for the still-necessary consumer-report function.

Note that this product research is done to protect the enterprise as a whole, and is not an essential cost of delivering a PC to a client. The enterprise benefits from this function *whether or not* it buys PCs from the IT department. Therefore, the consumer-report function should be funded on its own merits, as an enterprise expense — a Subsidy.

Consider another example: generating policies that ensure enterprisewide consistency in decision making or create synergies.

A marketing department may maintain standards on the enterprise logo and the appearance of its materials. Without these standards, the corporate identity would be weakened. Also, money might be wasted on many parallel design efforts. Marketing maintains these standards for the good of the enterprise, not for any one client.

Embedding the costs of designing and maintaining these standards in the price of client deliverables would distort rates upward, and business units might find that alternative sources of marketing services offer a better deal.

Another problem is that if these enterprise-good activities appear to be free (because their costs are hidden within the rates for other products and services), there may be a tendency to burden staff with too many such activities. Too often, enterprise initiatives are mandated without a clear understanding of their impacts on organizations' workloads and costs. By attaching a separate cost to these enterprise initiatives, executives can judge which are worthwhile and which are not.

Yet another problem with funding Subsidies through sales to clients is that it undermines the very intent of full cost recovery. Assigning enterprise costs to business units — which they don't control and don't need in order to operate — distorts business-unit profitability analyses.

Subsidies benefit the entire enterprise, and should be funded by the enterprise through direct budget, independent of clients' purchases. The profits that business units remit to the enterprise are used to fund the costs of the board of directors and the office of the CEO. They should also fund all the enterprise-good services coming from every internal service provider.

By the way, "mass-market" products and services that everybody in the enterprise buys — e.g., telephone, network, and email services provided by IT — may benefit everybody in the enterprise, but they are not eligible for Subsidy funding. These commodities are of value to the clients who buy them, as evidenced by their commercial availability; they are not strictly for the greater good. Thus, clients should be willing to pay for them.

To illustrate the difference, mass-market services like telephones and email are things that clients are willing to pay for. A Subsidy service, like enterprise policy facilitation, is something the board of directors may pay for, but individual business units have little interest in funding it.

Ventures

The second thing that should be funded by a direct budget, not imbedded in rates for products and services, is "Ventures" — *one-time funding for significant investments that improve an organization's effectiveness.*

One clear example is infrastructure (plant and equipment). "Infrastructure" means the assets that internal service providers own and operate in order to provide services to customers. [12]

Ventures include the following:

*   Capital for investments that will pay off over a term greater than one year, such as additions to infrastructure.

*   Significant research and development projects (distinct from ongoing training and product/service evolution, the costs of which are built into rates).

*   The start-up costs of new products and services.

*   Major improvements in an internal service provider's business, such as a transformation of its organization.

Venture projects aren't necessarily linked to specific enterprise strategies. They may replace or augment infrastructure. They may create new lines of business which produce value by delivering services at below-market costs. They may make organizations more efficient, effective, and competitive.

Where should the money to pay for your Ventures come from?

Not from clients!

To illustrate the problems caused by charging Ventures to clients, consider two actual case studies:

1. In a large entertainment company, the cost of IT infrastructure was funded as a component of applications-development projects, which clients paid for. They reasoned that this was equitable, and to some degree brought project cost-estimates closer to total life-cycle costs (although capital costs are only a portion of life-cycle costs of ownership).

    As a result, this company bought a new computer server (or a few) for each new IT application. After years of this practice, they found themselves running hundreds of servers, each supporting only one application, and most operating well below full capacity.

    To address this, they did a study which proved that the company could save millions of dollars each year by consolidating these servers (now called "virtualization").

    The justification was compelling. However, they ran into a not-so-surprising obstacle. Business units believed that they owned IT's servers. After all, they paid for them. Business-unit leaders wouldn't let IT consolidate "their" servers for fear of losing control, or of not having adequate capacity available when they needed it.

    Essentially, by asking clients to fund its infrastructure, this IT department had given away control of the assets they used to deliver services. This precluded enterprise capacity management.

2. A branch of the US Army provided another example. The IT department was required to break even (on a cash basis) each

year — again under the guise of full cost recovery. They bought a large mainframe computer near the end of one fiscal year, and were forced to raise the price of computer time in the last few months of that year to pay for it.

With this sudden, unexpected, and immense hike in rates, clients naturally questioned their IT costs and initiated an outsourcing study.

Clearly, funding for infrastructure should not come from clients, neither by direct charges nor allocations.

Another inappropriate source of funding for Ventures is "year-end money." This leaves funding for infrastructure and innovation to chance, betting on funds being left over at year-end to pay for critical investments in an organization's future.

How *should* these internal investments be funded?

Gifford Pinchot III proposed the concept of "intracapital" which would allow internal entrepreneurs to use the earnings from one success to fund the next venture. [13] While innovative, this idea didn't catch on, since few internal service providers make a profit; furthermore, the enterprise may redeploy the profits from one organization to another because it has better investment opportunities there; and a specific organization's need for Venture funding may not equal its profits.

In the real world, when a business needs to invest in infrastructure, new business ventures, or major improvements, it borrows money from a bank; and pays the bank back through a mortgage formula. These "mortgage" payments are embedded in the price of its products and services.

Similarly, every business within a business needs a bank to fund significant, one-time investments to improve their businesses within the business.

For a business within a business, the "bank" is the corporate treasury. Funding for Ventures should be supplied to an organization through its direct budget.

The enterprise is willing to loan the money because it expects its investment to pay off over time in the form of better, value-generating services to clients.

Funding for Ventures includes not only the capital, but all expenses required to ready the asset for use. Thus, capital budgets are not done in isolation, insensitive to the impacts on operating budgets. Coordinating capital investments with operating-expense budgets is essential to decision making, and also ensures that capital is not wasted for lack of the expense budget to implement and sustain it.

In addition, for new services, Venture funding includes losses incurred while service-volumes ramp up to a reasonable level of infrastructure utilization. This way, the first client to use a new service isn't saddled with its entire cost (and the next client thinks it's been paid and hence is free).

With these loans comes the obligation to pay back the bank, or at least to pay the depreciation on capital assets. Ideally, internal service providers should also pay interest on money employed, in-corporating the cost of capital in rates and decision making. These "mortgage payments" are then built into the rates for products and services. (Thus, clients ultimately pay the costs of Ventures, but over the life of the asset rather than all at once.)

To get funding from the bank, organizations must submit a proposal that justifies the investment (just like the proposal an external entrepreneur would present to banks or venture capitalists). Venture proposals describe the internal market (business need), and the value of the investment they propose to make across the enterprise. (They're rarely justified by the benefits of any specific client projects.)

Venture proposals are decided by each organization's chain of command and the enterprise's financial management processes. They are *not* decided by clients.

By treating these internal investments as distinct deliverables in an investment-based budget, corporate executives can explicitly analyze and decide these major investments based on their merits. This explicit decision process is far more fiscally sound and reliable than alternatives like embedding the cost in clients' projects, or hoping for a surplus of unknown size at year end.

Explicit funding also avoids the trap of clients thinking they own the organization's infrastructure, and empowers internal service providers to plan and manage their total capacity to meet the needs of the entire enterprise.

Funding for Innovation

Tight cost controls should not completely stifle innovation. Albeit at a reduced rate, innovation is essential in hard times as well as good.

To summarize the last two chapters, internal market economics provides funding for innovation in two ways:

For smaller and ongoing investments, internal entrepreneurs

include in their rates the necessary sustenance activities such as professional development, process improvement, and technology innovation. Since funding for these indirect costs vary in proportion to sales, the level of innovation and support remains in proportion to the overall size of the business.

Large, one-time investments have to be justified, like everything else in an organization's budget. Venture funding is the answer.

Case Example: Gaining Funding for Subsidies and Ventures

A lack of direct budget for Subsidies and Ventures puts an internal service provider at a serious competitive disadvantage, and quenches innovation.

In some organizations, an investment-based budgeting was the catalyst that reversed a "full cost recovery" mandate.

For example, Riverside County IT (RCIT) appeared more expensive than it actually was when the Board of Supervisors issued mandates that were not budgeted. RCIT had to embed in its rates the costs of delivering services such as policy facilitation, standards setting and compliance, and IT services to clients who weren't required to pay RCIT through chargebacks (such as the CEO's office and Board) — costs which should have been treated as Subsidies. [14]

Of course, these were costs that vendors and decentralized staff didn't bear. As a result, RCIT was often criticized for costing too much, and lost business when clients compared RCIT's rates to those of external vendors.

When they implemented investment-based budgeting, at first RCIT managers didn't want to bother splitting out these unfunded mandates, pessimistic that the County would change its ways. But Matt Frymire, CIO, insisted. The resulting cost model clearly documented the true cost of these enterprise-good deliverables.

With this evidence, the County auditors became allies in removing these costs from RCIT's rates. Frymire was able to convince the Board to provide direct budgets for these specific deliverables.

This was an important victory. Frymire won this battle because he had the facts, in the form of a transparent cost model underlying an investment-based budget.

Fall-back Options

In other cases, the policy can't be changed. What if the enterprise is adamant about full cost recovery, despite the problems it causes?

Even in these full-cost-recovery organizations, it's possible to mitigate the risks, provide an explicit channel of funding for Subsidies and Ventures, and keep the rates pure and comparable to external benchmarks.

There are three alternative means of funding Subsidies and Ventures with money that (unfortunately) comes from clients:

1. The Corporate Finance office can assess a tax on business units (an allocation), and use it to fund corporate activities including internal service providers' Subsidies and Ventures — just as funding is gathered for functions like the office of the CEO and CFO.

    This tax should be unrelated to what each business unit buys from the internal service providers. An allocation related to purchases essentially increases rates, with most of the same problems as imbedding these enterprise costs within rates. Instead, the allocation proportions should be based purely on the size of the business unit (e.g., its headcount, revenues, profits, or total budget).

In Figure 1, this is labeled "Separate Allocation."

2. The internal service provider itself can assess a tax on business units (a separate allocation), again based on a formula unrelated to what each business unit buys from it.

    This is less than ideal in that it forces the internal service provider to do the work of the Finance function, and gives it inappropriate power. It also invariably creates political noise that's unproductive. But at least it does not distort the organization's rates.

3. For Ventures, an internal service provider may borrow money from a business unit that's particularly interested in the service produced by those assets. It pays this loan back by discounting the price of those services. Rates are still calculated at full cost (including this depreciation). The repayment takes the form of a discount applied to invoices. Once the loan is fully repaid, rates remain the same and the discount is discontinued.

However, in no case should the cost of Subsidies and Ventures be imbedded in the costs of client deliverables in an investment-based budget or in rates. In that sense, even in a fee-for-service environment, "full cost recovery" is not a healthy goal.

IMPLICATIONS:

HOW THINGS WORK DIFFERENTLY

9. Cost Control

This section (Chapters 9 through 17) explore the impacts of internal market economics on some common challenges and concerns, explaining how they're treated differently (and more effectively) than with traditional business processes.

We start with an issue that's foremost on many executives' minds: cost control.

Internal market economics doesn't in any way diminish an enterprise's ability to control costs. In fact, it gives executives better tools to control costs more effectively than traditional financial processes.

Let's start by considering the disadvantages of conventional approaches to cost control, and then explore how internal market economics controls spending.

Traditional Cost Controls

In traditional approaches, executives control costs by limiting the budget provided to organizations.

The theory is that limiting an internal service provider's budget will control the enterprise's spending on that function. Using IT as an example, limiting the corporate IT department's budget is supposed to limit spending on information technology throughout the enterprise.

In reality, caps on internal service providers often drive costs up, not down. If business units need more IT, and if the corporate IT department doesn't have the resources to satisfy them, clients turn to alternatives such as decentralization and outsourcing, which are often more expensive and less effective. The truth is, capping an IT department's spending really only limits its market share.

When this loophole is discovered, some companies give the corporate IT department a monopoly in an attempt to stop spending on decentralization and outsourcing. Of course, it's very difficult to stop business units from spending their money on IT that way (other than obvious monopolies such as networking and the corporate ERP). Spending goes underground, with engineers and financial analysts doing IT work and vendors providing "professional services" rather than information services.

Even if people don't find ways to circumvent monopolies, arbitrary caps may preclude really good investments, including short-term investments which produce immediate cost savings elsewhere in the business.

Limiting supply is an extremely crude way to control costs.

Headcount Caps

In a similar vein, some companies limit the headcount of organizations. The intent is to stop foolish managers from hiring people to fulfill short-term demands, and then finding themselves with excess headcount when business volumes fall back to normal levels.

As long as managers hire only to the extent that long-term demands warrant and use staff augmentation contractors for short-term peak workloads, the only effect of headcount caps is to increase costs. They simply force organizations to use more expensive contractors and vendor services rather than hire employees when they're really needed.

Of course, if the cap applies to contractors as well, it has all the same problems as budget caps. It limits market share, not necessarily enterprise spending.

Inappropriate Use of the Budget Process

Another problematic means of cost control is to confuse budget planning with performance management. Instead of focusing on the best allocation of scarce resources, executives try to use budget cuts to force organizations to improve their productivity — to "do more with less."

It's obvious that organizations don't magically become more productive just because executives demand it. Organizations may become more efficient and rates may drop over time as a result of investments in process improvements. But at any given point in time, things cost what they cost. Demanding more for less doesn't change these facts.

Sadly, many executives cynically presume that managers won't improve their organizations unless they're pressured to do so by budget cuts.

In fact, budgeting is a poor venue for executive review of managers' performance-improvement objectives. Performance management should occur continually, not just once a year; and it's the job of leadership, not the budget process. It's naive to think that squeezing the budget is a fair substitute for ongoing performance management, or that doing so will lead to deliberate and well-planned process improvements.

Even if budget pressures do force productivity improvements, there's no reason to believe that this pressure will produce exactly the amount of savings required to meet the budget. That would be pure chance. Budget cuts are rarely based on facts like the estimated productivity gains to be expected from specific investments in process improvements.

More commonly, budget pressures often make organizations less, not more, productive. Robert's predicament illustrated the many reasons this happens.

Furthermore, when some organizations lack the resources to reliably deliver all they've promised, others who depend on them also become unreliable. Cutting budgets without consciously deciding what not to do causes things to fail randomly in various organizations throughout the enterprise. Ultimately, the entire enterprise becomes less capable of delivering even the important things, both operations and strategic initiatives.

Running an organization without internal market economics
is like steering a sailboat without a rudder.
You can give directions, but you can't be sure
where the organization will actually go.

John P. Gillispie
Executive Director - MOREnet
and former CIO, State of Iowa

A healthy budget process focuses strictly on allocating scarce enterprise resources in an optimal manner — a matter of deciding which activities to fund and which to forego — not on trying to command more productivity.

Controlling costs is done another way.

Cost Control in an Internal Market Economy

Internal market economics offers a far better way to control costs. Instead of attempting to control *supply*, executives control *demand*. Here's how it works:

Externally facing business units are required to either break even or meet profit targets. This limits how much they can spend on internal services — it controls demand.

In an internal market economy, internal service providers are not constrained by caps on their spending. They're free to expand supply to meet funded demand. They can hire contractors and vendors, as long as their revenues permit.

So what stops internal service providers from spending wastefully? Their costs are controlled in two ways:

1. They must break even. Internal service providers cannot spend more than their revenues allow (other than minor explainable variances, such as those caused by volume fluctuations which affect the recovery of indirect costs).

2. They must offer their products and services at better rates than their competition (decentralization and outsourcing). This stops them from building into their rates excessive costs.

Essentially, internal market economics breaks cost control into two distinct parts:

*   Customers must manage their demand, and not overspend their checkbooks. This means that checkbooks have to be tracked.

*   Suppliers must deliver fair value (competitive rates), and not overspend their revenues. This means that their revenues have to be tracked alongside their spending. (Traditional accounting systems only track spending.) And their rates have to be benchmarked.

I manage unit costs; you manage volumes.

Preston Simons
Corporate CIO
A Fortune 100 company

As long as customers are not allowed to buy more than they can pay for, and internal service providers are not allowed to incur costs beyond their revenues and are required to offer competitive rates, cost controls are comprehensive and effective.

There's no need for micro-management. There are no perverse incentives to circumvent caps. And by leaving performance management to bosses and the marketplace, executives are free to focus their attention during the budget process on aligning resources with the needs of the business, and on managing profit (or breakeven) targets rather than spending.

10. Downsizing

Despite efforts to control costs in a planned manner (Chapter 9), sometimes business conditions force a sudden downsizing. Here too, traditional approaches are unproductive and dangerous.

Spending Cuts

One approach is to tell managers to stop spending money.

Sometimes spending cuts target specific types of expenses, e.g., training, travel, or consulting budgets. Sometimes, all open (unfilled) positions are put on hold or eliminated.

Another variant is an across-the-board budget cut, leaving it to individual managers to decide how to trim spending.

Cutting costs this way reduces productive capacity, which translates into reduced quality and/or things not getting done. The critical issue is: Exactly what doesn't get done?

Traditional approaches leave it to individual managers to figure out how to cope with reduced resources.

The results are unfortunate:

*   When each manager independently tries to make ends meet, the selection of deliverables which don't get done is unpredictable and not driven by strategy.

*   When one manager cuts back on results in one area, others who need that group's help find themselves crippled. The result is a collapse of teamwork as one manager's highest

priority project is cut by another manager whose support services are critical to its success.

*   Critical sustenance activities are cut, and productivity and innovation deteriorate throughout the enterprise.

The core issue is this: Without executive coordination, results get cut in a haphazard way. With the impacts resembling a mosaic, a bit here and a bit there, virtually everything the enterprise does is crippled in some way. Ultimately, this makes the enterprise less capable of doing anything well enough to survive.

The long-term effects are insidious.

As people are disappointed with the support they (fail to) get from peers, staff gain a reputation for unreliability. Managers become reluctant to rely on peers. Teamwork is replaced with self-sufficient "stovepipe" organizations, where everybody is forced to work outside their domain of expertise. Quality suffers; redundancy is inevitable; productivity falls; and costs rise.

In the futile attempt to satisfy overwhelming demands with inadequate resources, managers forgo important investments in their own capabilities. They cut their own training, process improvements, and research. And they often burn out their staff with excessive workloads. This leads to short-term problems such as reduced productivity and turnover. It also leads to long-term problems such as a lack of planning and innovation, obsolete skills, and inadequate infrastructure. Again, costs go up.

Another unfortunate effect is that organizations miss great investments, even ones that might help the immediate cash-flow problem.

And worst of all, even the critical core functions necessary to the survival of the enterprise are compromised. Everything is affected, either directly or indirectly.

Slash and Burn

The slash-and-burn approach is even more drastic. A team of executives (perhaps with the help of external consultants) roams through the enterprise eliminating projects, cutting specific organizations' budgets, or even disbanding entire groups.

With the limited time such a task force has, they tend to "throw out the baby with the bath water." They make snap judgments about what's worth doing and what's not.

Entire projects are cut, when instead they might have been trimmed and refocused on the strategic objectives that caused them to be approved in the first place.

Entire groups are eliminated, when instead they might have been trimmed and refocused on just their really high-payoff deliverables.

As cuts are made and people are laid off, the enterprise loses competencies. The competencies it cuts are typically those needed to innovate and to grow, preserving only those functions needed in the short-term to operate what the enterprise has today.

Then, when the time comes for growth, the enterprise finds itself lacking the capabilities it needs to do new things. It's stuck in its smaller, strictly operational business. While it struggles to rebuild lost competencies, it's an easy target for competition.

Consider this example: [15]

A large aerospace manufacturing company faced a cash-flow crisis due to defense-spending cuts while they were in the midst of an expensive new-product introduction.

With their traditional resource-governance processes, top executives had little control over expenditures midway through the fiscal year. But they had to do something.

They began by building awareness of the problem in the hope that managers would voluntarily cut their spending. This had little impact, since everybody felt their programs were important enough to be continued.

Next, the top executives issued edicts. They cut all outside expenditures on training and consulting. This crippled some initiatives (including a few that were addressing the cash-flow crisis), but had only a small effect on the company's total spending since many managers found creative ways to fund the training and consulting they needed.

Ultimately, this firm had to resort to severe layoffs. An executive task force swept through the corporation, cutting every function by a significant percentage. Some functions that executives didn't understand were entirely eliminated, despite the cost savings they were producing and over the objections of their internal customers.

These cuts caused permanent damage to the firm's ability to compete. And when economic conditions improved, they were not able to grow. Once a leader in its industry, this corporation slid steadily downward until it was acquired by its competitor.

Strategic Cost Cutting in an Internal Market Economy

Traditional approaches may cut costs quickly. But they leave irreparable damage — an organization that stumbles in the short term, and isn't equipped to recover when conditions improve.

Clearly it's unwise to try to spread one's resources too thinly and do everything badly. Reducing budgets without revising downward the expectations of organizations is generally unsuccessful, damaging, and cruel.

The reality is that in a tough economy, an enterprise can no longer afford to do everything it had hoped or planned. The way to cut costs effectively is not to cut every organization's resources, but rather to *cut the enterprise's endeavors, and focus every organization on contributing all it can to those fewer deliverables.*

An internal market economy gives executives the ability to do exactly that.

In an investment-based budget, executives can see the total cost of all the various operational services and new initiatives. Instead of slashing total budgets and then letting things fail randomly (surgery with a butcher's axe), an investment-based budget allows executives to take a sober look at deliverables, and enables a business-driven decision process that eliminates products and services of marginal value (surgery with a scalpel).

When deliverables are cut, all the costs associated with those projects or services can be removed.

Once the direct costs of specific deliverables are cut, internal service providers reduce their indirect costs to appropriate levels given their now-smaller business volumes. They have to. If they don't, as their revenues fall, the amount of money built into rates to cover indirect costs won't be sufficient, so they'll generate a loss. Alternatively, if they increase their rates, they won't be competitive.

[Investment-based budgeting] helped us
make tough choices based on facts.
We didn't enjoy it, but it was better than
traditional across-the-board cuts.

Bernie Campbell
CIO
Sonoco Products Company [18]

Indirect cost cutting is best managed locally. Let those who really know what's critical and what's expendable — the managers of the organization itself — decide the cuts. As long as they're held accountable for breaking even and for competitive benchmarks, they'll have to rise to this challenge.

In summary, internal market economics suggests that executives *control demand (and let supply fall in place), in contrast with traditional approaches where executives cut supply directly.* When demand is cut and revenues are reduced, internal service providers have to cut their spending.

Whose job is it to cut demand?

It's unfair to hold internal service providers accountable for cuts.

For example, due to some unusual enterprise costs of a divestiture, cost cutting was required. The CIO was tasked with a big cut. But most of the Corporate IT organization's revenues came from chargebacks. The function was already very efficient, and recent benchmarks proved that. The only possibility was to cut back on services.

The question was, who was to decide which services would be cut? The Corporate CIO was put in the awkward position of being held accountable for, and hence having the authority to decide, the spending of his clients. Remember what happened when Robert began judging clients' needs and deciding his own priorities. It was unfair, and ultimately unproductive, to demand that this internal service provider force its clients to spend less.

When you look at why costs have gone up, you might find an inefficient internal service provider. But you're far more likely to discover that unit costs have trended down due to ever-increasing productivity, while the total cost of a service went up due to increased demand. In these cases, accountability for cost control clearly lies with pursers, not internal service providers.

The same is true of all demand — all projects and services. Customers, not suppliers, should be held accountable for reducing demand.

How can executives force customers to reduce their demand? It's easy: Reduce internal customers' spending power. That is, cut their checkbooks.

By focusing on cutting demand first and then removing just the related costs, an internal market economy channels resources to the few things the enterprise must do, and ensures that those few things are fully funded to ensure their effective delivery. It cuts costs without damaging an organizations' ability to deliver its most critical products and services.

It Could Have Been Worse: A Case Study

Riverside County, California, provides a poignant example of strategic cost cutting. [19]

By early 2009, Riverside County faced the third highest home-mortgage foreclosure rate in the State of California. Property values fell and unemployment rose to 11 percent. As a result, the County's property and sales tax revenues plummeted.

For Riverside County's IT department (RCIT), this meant deep cuts in its budget. CIO Matt Frymire was tasked with a 25 percent cut over three years, 10 percentage points of which had to occur immediately.

Frymire was caught between the proverbial rock and a hard place.

In organizations like RCIT that have been well managed in the past, there's no "low hanging fruit" and no way to "do more with less." For RCIT, budget cuts meant they'd do *less* with less. That's reality — the rock.

But meanwhile, clients (in this case, County agencies as well as local police and fire departments) needed IT to operate, and they continued to need all the services they received in the past — the hard place.

Of course, Frymire postponed any internal investments that weren't absolutely necessary. But the cuts were so deep that services had to be eliminated or service levels reduced.

Fortunately, in 2005, RCIT had implemented investment-based budgeting. [20]

"I can drill down and explain exactly what costs, direct and indirect, are in each rate," said RCIT financial analyst Debbie Zellner. "As an accountant with professional standards," she continued, "if we didn't have [investment-based budgeting], there's no way I could vouch for the numbers the way I do now."

Their investment-based budget gave Frymire the data and the credibility to enforce a strategic approach to cost cutting — a deliberate, business-driven process of deciding the "less."

First, Frymire went looking for marginal IT product lines. Investment-based budgeting gave him the ability to analyze profits and losses by product line. In doing so, he found a cost-savings opportunity.

RCIT had implemented a speech portal that provided telephone voice-recognition access to applications, a nice courtesy to tax-payers who could access County services by phone. Beyond just the obvious direct costs such as the vendor license and engineering staff, this speech portal drew on resources throughout the IT department. Investment-based budgeting revealed the true cost of the service.

However, only one agency used the service, so revenues were well below planned. "It was a nice service, but it wasn't cost-effective," Frymire said. "It was a luxury that the County just couldn't afford. We had to shut it down."

This decision alone saved the County hundreds of thousands of dollars in annual operating costs.

There were many other projects and services that would have to be cut to make the targeted savings. Frymire knew the decisions had to be made by clients, not him.

RCIT's account representatives routinely met with all the agencies each year to present a list of products and services and gain agreement on what would go into RCIT's budget. They repeated this process mid-year to accomplish this urgent cost-cutting objective. And clients made tough decisions.

After clients decided what they'd do without, RCIT used the cost model to remove only costs associated with those specific deliverables.

"We eliminated resources that worked on the projects and services we dropped," Zellner explained. Similarly, she managed vendor contracts based on the cost model, reducing spending where it was related to projects and services that were eliminated.

"We were able to cut costs fairly dramatically without jeopardizing our ability to keep the enterprise running," Frymire reported.

Clients reacted well despite a reduction in IT services. "They understand that RCIT is doing everything it can to ensure they continue to receive critical services during these tough budget times," Zellner reported.

"I don't know if we were far-sighted or just lucky to have implemented [investment-based budgeting] when we did," Frymire reflected, "but it sure paid off for us during this budget crisis."

11. Shared Services, Mergers, and Acquisitions

The term "shared services" can be applied to almost any function in an enterprise. It's most commonly used to describe internal service providers like IT, HR, finance, facilities, administrative services, etc.; but engineering, manufacturing, marketing, and sales are also internal services provided to product managers who are accountable for the profit-and-loss of the products and services sold externally. Every functional area serving those externally facing product managers is a shared service.

Shared services can also refer to organizations at any level of the enterprise. For example, corporate functions serve corporate users and all business units. Business unit functions serve all the departments within a business unit. And departmental functions serve all the users within the department. All are shared services.

In essence, any organization is a shared service if it produces products and services for others within the enterprise.

Consolidation of Internal Service Functions

Some people use the phrase "shared services" as a euphemism for consolidation (centralization).

Consolidation results in both economies of scale and synergies. [21] Redundancies are eliminated. Larger consolidated organizations can afford a higher degree of specialization, which leads to lower costs, improved performance, and more innovation. Consolidation of buying power also brings costs down.

Consolidation doesn't mean that "one size fits all." A well-managed shared-services organization can (if it's entrepreneurial) produce custom solutions to satisfy the unique needs of specific clients more efficiently and effectively than decentralized staff.

Even when producing custom solutions, shared services can save money by standardizing components. For example, when multiple product managers buy support from a shared engineering function, the variety of nuts and bolts in the parts bin is typically reduced.

Consolidation of shared services may also produce enterprisewide synergies. For example, that common parts bin may reveal opportunities for shared components and for interoperability, which enhance the value of all the products.

Using IT as another example, consolidation may deliver business synergies through better information sharing, common business processes, and cross-boundary collaboration.

Internal Market Economics Drives the Right Relationships

For shared services to succeed, internal service providers must earn the position of clients' vendor of choice. If they don't, the pendulum eventually swings back to decentralization.

First and foremost, this means treating clients as customers — not as "users" who must take whatever you decide to give them, or even as "business partners" with muddled accountabilities.

A critical component of customer focus is empowering clients to decide what they buy. Internal market economics does exactly that, during the budget process and throughout the year (regardless of whether the shared-services organization receives budget directly or via chargebacks). As a result, clients should be no more threatened by shared services than they are by the external vendors they use. It's not a win-lose situation.

I'd rather have a customer than a hostage.

Preston Simons
Corporate CIO
A Fortune 100 company

Being clients' vendor of choice also means delivering products and services that are competitive in quality and price. This requires an accurate cost model that gets all the indirect costs in the right places and permits competitive benchmarks.

Internal market economics also sets up the right culture. It encourages managers to be entrepreneurial, offering an up-to-date catalog of products and services at competitive prices, delivering on all their promises, and treating customers like customers.

Furthermore, internal market economics enhances relationships, making clients comfortable with shared services.

Implementing internal market economics is an essential step in establishing and growing shared-services organizations.

Mergers and Acquisitions

In mergers and acquisitions, the integration challenges are very similar. Multiple organizations provide similar services. Just like shared-services consolidations, the cost savings and synergies that justify the merger or acquisition depend on a successful integration of these parallel functions.

Steps in a Successful Integration Process

The safest approach to consolidations, and to merger and acquisition integrations, is a three-step process. (See Figure 3.)

Figure 3: Three-step Consolidation Process

1. **Consolidation:** move the reporting lines, but leave groups intact; don't break anything!
2. **Integration:** deconstruct and then merge the products/ services within groups; best done as a participative process.
3. **Optimization:** realize the synergies by eliminating redundancies and following best practices within each line of business.

First, join the multiple organizations under a common executive, leaving them operating as they were. (Don't break anything.) This gives the executive legitimate authority to engage the expanded management team in the integration process.

Then, the next step is integration. This should not be a matter of "winners" dominating "losers." Cost savings and synergies depend on combining similar functions and capitalizing on the best of breed, regardless of source.

Furthermore, it's not wise to jam together groups with similar sounding titles. The only accurate way to decide what goes where is to involve all the leaders in identifying the products and services each group delivers and the resources associated with each. Then, the specific deliverables within each group, and associated resources, can be sorted out and integrated (rather than moving groups, which may be multi-functional, in their entireties).

A fair selection process for leadership positions in the new organization completes this principles-based integration process.

Once integration is complete, the third and final step is optimization. Managers of the now-combined groups extract the cost savings and generate the synergies. This step may take months or years, as managers blend and evolve processes and gain the advantages of their combined strengths.

Role of Internal Market Economics

Note that this approach parallels the implementation process for internal market economics. Specifically, the investment-based budgeting process includes the following steps:

1. Deconstruct groups into "lines of business" using a consistent framework. Some managers may have more than one line of business under them.

2. Define each line of business' catalog of products and services. This shows where products and services overlap with a clarity far beyond just the labels in boxes on an organization chart, and provides the data for the integration step.

3. Define each line of business' commitments (projects and services) as "sales" of those catalog items. This documents each group's commitments so that no balls are dropped.

4. Associate all costs (not just direct costs) with those sales. The result is both an investment-based budget (cost of each sale) and a catalog with rates.

    Assisting with the optimization phase, rates show which practices are "best of breed" within each line of business.

And the cost model reveals assets and expenses which can be shared — costs linked to the same products and services.

Throughout this process, collaboration is well structured. The investment-based budgeting process provides a basis for participation that's fact-based, not a battle of opinions.

With documented frameworks, a well-structured process, and open participation, an integration process can attain its promised synergies and savings, build morale, and establish an entrepreneurial culture — all at the same time.

Costs of Decentralization

Once shared services are consolidated, some business units may later want to re-establish decentralized functions.

The leader of a recently consolidated state government data center faced such a challenge. Some rogue state agencies insisted that they'd be better off not buying from the new data center.

Using the cost model and their investment-based budget, the data center was able to calculate the increase in costs to all other state agencies if this one agency withdrew its business, reducing the economies of scale that were benefitting all agencies. That evidence generated peer pressure which, along with the dissenting agency's inability to calculate its own decentralized costs, quashed the rebellion.

Decentralization almost always costs more. When it does, internal market economics reveals the facts, which should preclude dismembering shared services for the wrong reasons.

12. Expert Stewardship

Some staff feel that because they're experts in their professions, they should be the ones making decisions about their domains. They feel it's their job to protect the best interests of the enterprise as "stewards" of their technologies and resources.

These people think of customers as "unruly children" whom they need to control on behalf of the enterprise. They sponsor projects and decide their own priorities, and sometimes unilaterally make policy decisions. They may honestly believe that they know what's best for you!

This definition of stewardship is, of course, the opposite of customer focus. It undermines an organization's culture, disempowers its customers, and certainly does not lead to the best decisions about the allocation of scarce resources.

Contributing Expertise Without Disempowering Customers

It's true; internal service providers know their professions. It's equally true that clients know their businesses. And it takes both bodies of knowledge to make the right decisions.

In the original Star Trek, Vulcans like Mr. Spock were capable of a "mind meld." Placing his fingertips on your temples, Spock's mind and yours would merge, and you'd share one another's thoughts and knowledge. If clients and suppliers could meld their minds this way, integrating clients' knowledge of their businesses with suppliers' knowledge of their products and services, the right decisions would emerge.

But lacking a Vulcan mind meld, one party must share all it knows, and the other party must then make a decision.

Internal service providers could study the needs of their clients, and then decide for them what products and services to provide. But then it wouldn't be fair to hold clients accountable for the results of their businesses, since decisions about key factors of production are being made by others.

A customer-focused internal service provider works the other way around. It shares all it knows with its clients, and then respects their decisions about what they purchase from it.

For example, in response to a customer's business need, an internal entrepreneur suggests alternatives (like "Chevrolet, BMW, Rolls-Royce"). For each alternative, the supplier shares everything the customer needs to know to make an informed decision: costs, time required, pros and cons, risks, required variances from standards, differences in customers' accountabilities, etc.

With this information, customers can choose alternatives within the context of their unique insider knowledge of their businesses.

At times, customers may choose an alternative that would not have been the supplier's first choice. The customer may choose a Chevrolet, when suppliers know that a Rolls-Royce is an investment that lasts for generations (and is much more fun to build). But suppliers must remember that their customers have been appointed to run their businesses, and are held accountable for the results of those businesses. The choices they make are the ones they perceive will most benefit their businesses.

(The customer who deliberately makes choices that are not in the best interests of his/her business is a special case, and hopefully a rare one. This is a management matter, not a resource-governance issue. When misbehavior becomes evident, it should be escalated. But internal service providers' staff should not be encouraged to judge their customers' decisions, a practice which will undermine their customer focus and effective resource governance.)

Limits to Customer Authorities

Respecting customers' right to decide what they buy doesn't mean that suppliers just do as they're told. There are limits to customers' authorities.

While customers are qualified to decide *what* they buy, *how* those products and services are made must be left to the suppliers who are in the best position to know, and are accountable for producing those deliverables.

There's another limit to customers' authorities that's important to note. When internal service providers buy infrastructure for the purpose of providing services to customers, they own those assets. Asset owners are fully responsible for the safekeeping, appropriate use, and returns on investments in those assets. Therefore, internal service providers have every right to decide what they'll buy (as long as they can justify the investment), and to set the rules about how their infrastructure will be used.

Clear Mutual Accountabilities

Internal market economics defines customers' and suppliers' accountabilities clearly: Customers choose what they buy. Suppliers choose how to make it.

With the authority to make choices comes accountability for

results. Customers are accountable for their businesses, for buying what they need, and for making good use of what they buy. Suppliers are accountable for offering the best deal, and for delivering on every commitment with quality.

Internal market economics makes the best use of everybody's expertise. It matches authorities with accountabilities. And it leads to respectful and productive partnerships.

The Meaning of "Stewardship"

In fact, stewardship is not at all counter to customer focus.

Stewardship means proactively putting forward alternatives and sharing your knowledge, as long as you don't cross the line and make customers' purchase decisions for them.

Once customers decide what they'll buy, it means delivering those products and services with professional excellence. This includes providing great quality at a fair price, and building in everything the customer needs to make the intended use of the product or service. (E.g., cars come with air in the tires.)

Stewardship doesn't mean knowing what's best for others or making their purchase decisions for them. It means taking the best possible care of the business that's been entrusted to you, which includes being the best possible supplier to your customers.

13. Outsourcing

Many of the products and services produced by internal service providers can be purchased from vendors, i.e., outsourced. Outsourcing includes off-shore contractors, as well as vendors' products and services (e.g., in IT, cloud computing).

There are cases where outsourcing is more economic, and cases where it's not. [22] Internal market economics encourages people to make optimal use of vendors, and avoid the mistake of outsourcing for the wrong reasons or when the economies aren't there.

When to Use Outsourcing

On the surface, one would think that paying other shareholders a profit to do what you're already doing at break-even wouldn't save money. But there are circumstances where external vendors can produce products and services less expensively or better than internal providers.

Specifically, external vendors are more cost-effective when:

* There are economies of scale which cross corporate boundaries; that is, when multiple corporations can share a vendor's assets. An obvious example is telecommunication networks, where many corporations and individuals buy service from the same vendors and share long-distance telecommunications lines.

* Due to its size, a vendor can afford a higher degree of specialization. This is of particular value in highly specialized professions where only the largest organizations can afford to

hire a qualified individual. In this case, outsourcing means bringing in specialized consultants as needed.

This criterion may extend to a regional market, or to a specific specialty. It may even extend to a particular product or service. For example, a specific product or service, or level of service, may have volumes so low that the organization cannot afford to produce it internally.

* A company requires more capital than is available to it; so it's willing to pay a premium in operating expenses to use other companies' assets.

* Business volumes vary dramatically, or grow more quickly than an organization can hire staff and acquire resources. So it's worth paying more to make costs variable rather than fixed.

In these situations, the benefits warrant paying a vendor its profit margin.

When Not to Use Outsourcing

On the other hand, there are situations where outsourcing may appear tempting, but it's a poor choice:

* Focus on core competencies.

Some say an enterprise should "stick to its knitting" and outsource everything other than the heart of its business, its core competencies. The truth is, after outsourcing, they wind up with no additional employees doing the "knitting" than they'd had when support functions were supplied internally.

And it's certainly not the case that managing a vendor is easier than managing an executive of an internal service provider. All the lawyers and consultants who specialize in outsourcing will confirm that.

Focusing on core competencies is a fallacious justification for outsourcing.

* Outsourcing may be a better value than an inefficient internal service provider.

However, it's generally far preferable to fix the internal service provider yourself rather than throw money at a vendor to take the problem off your hands. Using outsourcing in this situation locks the enterprise into an approach that, in the long term, will be more expensive and less flexible than a healthy internal service provider.

Outsourcing is a Tool, Not a Goal

Of course, outsourcing is not an end in itself. It makes no sense to ask the question, "What are all the things we can outsource?" The literature is rife with companies that have outsourced entire functions, only to find themselves struggling to regain control and rebuild internal capabilities.

Rather than pursue outsourcing as a goal, organizations should continually look for the optimal mix of vendors, contractors, and employees.

How can an organization know when outsourcing is appropriate? Said another way, how can you make just the right use of vendors?

The Outsourcing Study

A common, but ineffective, way to decide on outsourcing is to analyze an entire function such as IT, facilities, or customer service. If it appears that internal costs are too high, the entire function is turned over to a vendor.

Such studies aggregate internal costs into high-level categories (perhaps called "towers"), and then compare costs with data on past outsourcing contracts in other companies.

As Robert pointed out, this can be very misleading. Among the many questions such comparisons raise, consider these:

*   Are there attributes of your business (such as location or market niche) that drive higher costs, whether internal or outsourced?

*   Are you forced to spend more due to your company's strategy, or to laws or regulations?

*   Are you spending more because you've found ways to make better use of internal services to leverage your business?

*   Are you more expensive because you haven't invested in improvements, such that an internal investment would offer a better return than outsourcing?

*   Are your service-levels really comparable, or do you need more, or a higher quality, of services than the other companies in the database.

Studies which compare your spending to others in your industry have all the same problems. And in addition, you can't buy from your competitors; so even if they're cheaper, the comparison provides no realistic opportunity to reduce costs.

Furthermore, neither of these high-level cost comparisons gives you data in sufficient detail to know where cost-savings opportunities can be found.

The implication of these studies is that it's an all-or-nothing decision. Instead of selectively buying from vendors when appropriate, it compares the costs of outsourcing entire functions (or major portions of them).

It's extremely dangerous to outsource an *entire* function. This wastes money if your internal service provider is very cost effective at many of its products and services, and only a few are candidates for outsourcing.

Worse, it leaves critical decisions (like policies, priorities, and spending controls) to people who are morally obliged to optimize the profits of other shareholders. Of course, they'll talk about partnership and how their success depends on your success (all true). But at the end of the day, if there's any discrepancy between their profits and yours, you know which must win.

For example, imagine a situation where a $2 million project would produce benefits of $2.5 million, a 25% return on the investment. Alternatively, a $500,000 project would solve many of the same problems and produce a $1 million benefit, a 100% return on the investment.

Although the smaller investment is clearly a better deal, an outsourcing vendor's staff is obligated to look after the best interest of its shareholders first, and would have to recommend the higher-cost/lower-return option.

Fair Comparisons

Internal market economics provides a much better basis for deciding when to use vendors' services.

Rates set with a good cost model help ensure that comparisons are fair. Indirect costs are apportioned to just the right deliverables. Enterprise costs (Subsidies and Ventures) are excluded. Rates are accurate, believable, and comparable to market costs.

If a vendor offers a price on a subset of what you do, you can isolate the internal cost of that same subset of your deliverables.

If they offer a lower quality of service, you can isolate your costs for that same service level.

With accurate cost data on internal products and services, specific internal products and services can be compared fairly to outsourcing alternatives over the life of the proposed vendor contract.

Case Example

Riverside County IT (RCIT) provides a great example. [23] County departments are required to use RCIT for some services such as networking and the data center. But for optional services such as applications development and hosting, many departments had their own decentralized IT staff, and also bought directly from vendors.

RCIT would bid for these optional services. But its rates were not comparable with outside bids, and often weren't competitive.

One problem was a lack of granularity in its rates. The IT budget had been built around very broad activities. The telecommunications rates, for example, covered the cost of the entire network;

they were not broken out by the individual services that the network provided.

In one case, the Sheriff's department acquired a new server and wanted RCIT to support it. They were charged for the full range of data center services, including 24x7 support, whether they needed them or not.

"They were providing services, but not necessarily the services that our department was looking for," said John Naccarato, of the Riverside County Sheriff's Department. "That caused us to go outside, seek bids, and [by paying vendors a profit] pay more for those services in the long term."

Another problem was in the calculation of those rates. Costs were put into large pools, which were spread into some (or all) rates.

"Our customers didn't know what was included in the rates. And to be quite honest, we didn't either," said Matt Frymire, Riverside County's CIO. Since rates were not based on a transparent cost model, clients lost trust in RCIT's rate structure.

What clients wanted was a catalog with clear rates associated with each service, and the flexibility to pick and choose the services they wanted. But remember, services were defined in big bundles; customers were paying for services they did not use; the rates weren't right; and no one understood them.

Beginning in the spring of 2005, the RCIT management team worked together to design their catalog, implement an investment-based budget, and calculate rates.

When the new catalog and rates came out, it raised some concerns. Some rates went up and others went down, since costs were now assigned to just the right products and services. With the new, more accurate rates, some departments were paying less for IT, while others were paying more.

At first, Naccarato was shocked by the new rates. But the transparent cost model paid off. "When we ask about a certain rate, our RCIT account manager can explain it now," Naccarato said. He ultimately agreed that the rates were justifiable and fair.

Beyond just equity, the process made it clear when RCIT's services could best be used, and when it made more sense for the Sheriff's department to look outside for services. "We can judge if prices are competitive or not; so we're in a much better position to make sound business decisions," Naccarato said.

The good news is that the Sheriff's department continued to use the RCIT services they had been using, even though some of the costs went up. With the right granularity in its rates, RCIT turned out to be very competitive.

RCIT continued to improve as it scrutinized its business in ways it never could before. with detailed and accurate rates, RCIT benchmarked its costs against the private sector. Where the rates were out of line, they determined the best solution: outsourcing, or improving their processes to deliver a service more effectively. This illustrates the concept of "strategic sourcing."

Strategic Sourcing

Beyond just supplying fair benchmarks, internal market economics continually optimizes the use of vendors. Here's how it works:

Every manager at every level of the organization strives to be the vendor of choice to his/her customers. A key part of that is offering the best value.

In practice, every vendor and consultant in the world can be considered part of the staff of an internal entrepreneurship.

If a vendor offers a product or service at a price or quality that's better than that which can be produced internally, an internal entrepreneur should be the first to suggest it. Entrepreneurs choose "buy" over "make" (utilizing vendors instead of staff) whenever it's more economical to do so. This is how they can always offer the best price and maintain their market share.

The IT department at Sonoco Products Company exemplifies this. "We continually compare internal rates versus external," said Bernie Campbell, CIO. "When sustainable external services can be procured at lower rates, we outsource. But for the most part we've found that fully-burdened internal rates are less expensive for critical services like internal consulting, architecture, and the PMO." [24] For Sonoco's data center, however, outsourcing turned out to be a better choice.

Unlike outsourcing entire functions, vendors are only used where they offer better value, termed "strategic sourcing."

Instead of being stuck with a big, multiyear contract, the balance of internal and vendor resources can be adjusted flexibly as shifting economics dictate. Market forces will automatically and continually seek the optimal use of vendor services.

Even if most of a function is outsourced, an internal organization should manage those vendors. This is more than a procurement role. The internal function should decide its catalog of products and services, plan its budget, make commitments to internal clients, and manage vendors as part of its delivery capability.

This way, the enterprise benefits from employees — people who know the function and who work for your shareholders — retaining full accountability for delivering products and services to their customers, whether they make, buy, or a blend of the two. People you can trust are the ones who decide policies, advise the business on its best choices, and ensure that vendors perform as promised.

Treatment of Costs

With strategic sourcing, the catalog of products and services offered internally does not have to match the deliverables provided by the outsourcing vendors. In fact, in most cases, it should not.

For example, an outsourcing vendor may charge an internal IT department for technical deliverables like computer servers, CPUs and memory capacity, and monitoring. But an internal IT department may apply all these costs (along with some internal costs) to the simpler, more understandable services in its catalog such as applications hosting and email.

Thus, whether they're a large or small component of your cost structure, outsourcing vendors' are just another cost to be apportioned to your products and services through a cost model.

14. Unfunded Mandates

From time to time, executives demand that organizations deliver additional work, but don't provide incremental funds.

In government, this results from legislative mandates without associated funding.

In companies, the same thing happens. Special circumstances such as acquisitions, regulatory changes, and disasters require special actions. But the problem is, budgets may not be augmented.

Reality: Mandating Doesn't Make Things Free

Obviously, unfunded mandates don't give an organization the ability to produce more than resources permit. Mandates consume resources that would otherwise be devoted to something else.

Organizations may do their best to rise to the challenge. But inevitably, many things suffer. Staff cut corners on quality, come in late, or fail to deliver entirely on commitments they've made to their customers. And just like across-the-board cuts, things fail randomly across the enterprise, with unpredictable results.

When looked at through the lens of internal market economics, internal service providers who divert resources from planned activities to unfunded mandates are essentially stealing from clients' checkbooks in order to serve executives.

Another response, hardly better, is to sacrifice training and innovation. One may think this is only to satisfy a temporary, short-term exigency. But the truth is, it's a slippery slope. Do it once and you'll reinforce the belief that your organization can absorb more work without more resources. It'll be expected again and again. Eventually, there will never be enough time for anything but working directly on urgent projects. Of course, this is myopic. Doing without these necessary sustenance activities is only postponing your inevitable demise.

However an organization manages to do them, the costs of mandates ultimately appear in clients' bills and in organizations' budgets. So organizations look more expensive than they really are.

How Internal Market Economics Funds Mandates

Special circumstances may impact priorities throughout an enterprise; but unfunded mandates should never force organizations to promise more than they can deliver, or force them to steal from one client in order to satisfy another.

Internal market economics suggests a better way: *An unfunded mandate forces the hand of pursers, not suppliers.* Pursers have to spend their precious checkbooks on things that may not have been their chosen priorities.

With the mandate forced to the top of the priority stack, pursers have to think carefully about what to do with the remaining funds in their checkbooks. Naturally, they'll choose to eliminate the lowest-value projects and services.

This way, adjustments to priorities are explicit, not random. Scarce resources continue to flow to the most important priorities. And organizations won't fail to meet their commitments due to "unfunded" mandates.

15. Management Metrics and Internal Controls

Internal market economics has some signification implications for the way we measure managers.

A closely related topic is internal controls. Just as the national economy depends on the rule of law, internal controls are required for market economics to work inside organizations.

Controls are needed to ensure the integrity of the marketplace:

*   Controls are needed to prevent theft and fraud.

*   Pursers can't spend more than their checkbooks permit. Controls insure the integrity of checkbooks,

*   Controls are needed to insure that suppliers don't spend more than their revenues permit, and offer competitive rates.

*   Internal customer-supplier contracts must be respected. Controls reinforce the integrity of commitments.

Internal market economics gives managers the authority to make decisions; accountability for controls goes along with that empowerment.

Traditional Metrics: Spending Control

Traditional financial controls track whether managers spend no more than they'd planned. If costs exceed planned, termed a "negative variance," they're expected to explain themselves.

This incents the wrong behaviors. It tells managers not to spend more than is in the budget, even if additional costs are justifiable;

and it condones spending within budgeted limits even if those costs aren't needed.

Here's an illustration:

* Jane is entrepreneurial and grows her shared-services business by delivering great value. Her revenues grow as customers discover new ways to benefit from her services and supply incremental funding to buy more from her.

  Of course, as revenues grow, her expenses grow. Traditional metrics would portray this as a negative variance — expenses exceeding planned. Jane has to explain her spending. A hero comes into question for succeeding.

* John is a poor performer and produces very little, but spends just what he said he'd spend. John has no variance to explain.

Fear of variances may cause internal service providers to send clients to outsourcing vendors or to encourage decentralization, rather than expand their businesses and risk budget variances.

Also, this metric does little to build a culture of accountability for results. Remember, John produced very little, but looked good.

Even worse, some traditional variance reports track spending by general-ledger expense-code. As business needs change and clients adjust their priorities, managers may need to spend more on one type of expense and less on another — e.g., more on vendor services and less on consulting.

However, tracking variances at the expense-code level forces managers to be inflexible (or to cheat). They may even spend more than is needed on consulting (using the above example) just because the budget allows it, which wastes money.

Meanwhile, if they spend less than is needed on another type of expense (vendor services, in the above example), they reduce their capability to deliver needed results.

Another way traditional spending controls encourage waste is that if managers don't spend their entire budgets by the end of the year, their budgets may be reduced in subsequent years. This "use it or lose it" practice leads to a scramble to "get rid of" year-end money, spending it on things that may not be worthwhile.

Internal Market Economics Metrics: Spending Control

Internal market economics suggests a new set of metrics to control spending. It's simple: Costs should not exceed revenues, as portrayed in a profit-and-loss (P&L) statement.

Jane is a hero for bringing in more business, while still breaking even. John is in trouble, having produced little revenues while incurring all the planned expenses.

It's a matter of managing people to their bottom lines, not their top lines — to break-even (or profit targets), not spending caps.

There's certainly no need to track spending by expense-code. With internal market economics, managers are considered successful if total spending is no more than their revenues. And they're empowered to spend what they must in any expense category to deliver their products and services as efficiently as possible.

Also, with investment-based budgeting, there's no incentive to spend all that's in the budget since next year's budget will be based on clients' purchase decisions rather than this year's spending.

Value: Benchmarking

In addition to spending limits, managers should be measured on value — whether or not they're a good deal.

With rates based on fully burdened costs, managers can be measured by competitive benchmarks: their rates compared to vendor prices for equivalent services.

Unlike high-level statistics such as total spending on a function or gross costs by high-level category, rate comparisons answer the question, "Can I buy the same product or service for less money elsewhere?" This is the most accurate and meaningful form of benchmarking.

This metric provides an incentive to eliminate any unnecessary spending, and to operate as efficiently as possible, including optimizing internal processes and using vendors (strategic sourcing) whenever it will bring rates down.

By the way, benchmarks can be a powerful marketing tool for internal service providers who offer better rates than vendors and decentralized suppliers. Even if there are some specific areas that need improvement, the openness builds trust and usually buys managers time to improve and beat their competition.

Internal market economics employs measurement as both a management tool (to direct internal decisions) as well as a communications vehicle (to describe the value delivered in terms meaningful to customers).

Len Bergstrom
Senior Vice President
Real Decisions/Gartner

Cost of Capital

Joel Stern and Bennett Stewart pointed out that managers' contributions to shareholder value must account for the costs of capital they employ. [25] They proposed a management metric that they called "Economic Value Added"[R] (EVA), net operating profit after tax minus the opportunity cost of invested capital.

With internal market economics, special processes to calculate EVA aren't needed. If an enterprise charges interest on the capital managers employ (working capital as well as assets), then return-on-assets will be incorporated into every manager's rates and P&L. [26] Without this interest requirement, internal service providers have an unfair competitive advantage over vendors; and as they grow, they dilute the enterprise's returns-on-assets.

Billable-time Ratios

Of course, it's not right to meet one's financial objectives by abusing one's staff. Financial metrics can be complemented with a metric of "billable-time ratios" — the percentage of time spent on deliverables for customers rather than sustenance tasks.

Too low a ratio means that too much is being spent on sustenance activities, ultimately leading to a financial loss or high rates.

On the other hand, too high a ratio may produce favorable financials, but at the expense of staff training, process improvements, innovation, customer relations, and other critical sustenance tasks. In time, this seriously damages the organization and its staff.

Appropriate billable-time ratios should be determined for each unique business within a business, i.e., for each line of business

under each manager. Then, hitting those targets should be part of
every manager's performance metrics.

Customer Satisfaction

In an entrepreneurial organization, metrics can go beyond just the
numbers. All managers can be evaluated on customer satisfaction
because they have clearly defined customers.

Internal entrepreneurs can also be measured by their "market
share" — the percentage of enterprisewide spending on a function
that goes to the shared-services provider rather than decentralization and outsourcing. Ultimately this is the most comprehensive
indicator of performance.

---

*[The successful organization of the future] will be ... composed largely of
specialists who direct and discipline their own performance through
organized feedback from colleagues, customers, and headquarters.*

Peter F. Drucker [27]

Balanced Metrics

Based on internal market economics, a new suite of metrics
balances cost control (breaking even) and entrepreneurship
(delivering value to the enterprise).

Metrics focus on results rather than how people deliver those
results, fundamental to empowerment. They give managers flexibility and room to innovate within the bounds of clear objectives.

And metrics encourage managers to please customers, and to
invest in staff and in sustainable businesses.

16. The Executive Bottleneck [29]

When a company is young, its founder has a pretty good handle on what everybody is doing. He/she personally meets with all the managers and sets priorities. He/she coordinates the various functions, establishing teams and pointing out interdependencies. He/she is involved in many operational decisions. The top executive is often the glue that holds the company together.

As companies grow, one person can no longer know enough to coordinate the activities of the entire enterprise. The time and "brain cycles" of the founder are stretched to the limit.

The same is true of internal service providers. As they grow (in parallel with the growth of the enterprise or through consolidations of shared services), at some point the executive in charge faces precisely the same challenges.

When size and complexity has grown to the point where one individual can no longer personally know everything that's going on in every corner of the organization, ironically, the leader who successfully grew the organization may become the constraint to its continued success.

Worse, he/she may be involved in decisions that subordinates are better equipped to make. As a result, mistakes are made, and strong leaders at the next tier may be driven away.

Meanwhile, an executive immersed in operational details doesn't have enough time to focus on the strategic decisions and external relationships where he/she is most needed.

When its top executive can no longer keep up with everything going on every day, an organization inevitably must transition from an executive-controlled small group to a well-managed team.

The way this transition is handled determines whether or not the organization will continue to grow while preserving the entrepreneurial character that made it successful in the first place.

Internal market economics has much to contribute to an organization or a company that's "growing up."

The Solution: Three Legs of the Stool

To eliminate the bottleneck at the top and refocus the executive on strategic issues, like three legs of a stool, three things are needed:

Leg 1:   The top executive must learn to manage through others, and to focus his/her personal attention on strategic challenges (or step aside).

Leg 2:   Senior leaders at the next level must evolve from functional experts to business leaders.

Leg 3:   Senior leaders must be empowered to run their respective organizations.

Leg 1 is well understood. In start-up companies, some founders are able to grow into the role of enterprise executives. For those who do not, it's not uncommon for a board of directors to replace (or complement) the founder with a "professional manager."

Leg 2 is also well understood. Some leaders are insightful enough to engage executive coaches. [30] Some take advantage of leadership development programs. And in some cases, seasoned executives are hired into senior leadership positions. Internal market economics can contribute to this learning process.

Leg 3 is the most difficult challenge, and is effectively addressed by internal market economics.

Leg 3: Discipline Without Bureaucracy

To tap all the talent that's already in the organization, the next tier of leaders must be empowered to manage their respective groups, exercise their creativity, and work directly with one another — without the need for day-to-day involvement of the top executive.

Don't tell people how to do things;
tell them what to do and let them surprise you with their results.

George S. Patton

However, empowerment cannot mean chaos. Everyone must be aligned with strategies; resources must be controlled; and activities must be coordinated — functions formerly done by the top executive.

Disciplined business processes must take the place of an individual at the top personally controlling resources and coordinating everybody's activities.

Key to a successful transition is installing control and coordination processes without destroying the entrepreneurial culture. If these processes are badly designed, organizations become bureaucratic and ineffective.

The answer to this conundrum — discipline without bureaucracy — can be found in internal market economics.

With internal market economics, managers can be empowered to run their organizations as they see fit. They become entrepreneurs who strive to earn their internal and external customers' business by offering the right products and services, excellent value, and a customer-focused culture. To do so, they manage their costs, deliver on promises, innovate, and team with peers and vendors to optimize their value propositions.

From my perspective as a CEO,
having empowered internal entrepreneurs
promotes healthy, long-term shareholder value.

Sergio A. Paiz
CEO
PDC Group

Meanwhile, managing their internal entrepreneurships develops the business acumen of the leaders (contributing to Leg 2). Those who embrace the entrepreneurial environment and learn to run a business within a business become the next generation of enterprise leaders. This may avoid the need for some of the familiar turnover that often accompanies growth — a waste of the talent and knowledge that's critical to an organization's continued success.

There's no need to worry about a loss of control with this kind of empowerment. Financial controls are comprehensive (as described in Chapter 9). And with internal market economics, clear deliverables and objective metrics help executives hold managers accountable for both results and financial performance.

In many ways, top executives are in better control of the business than when they were personally immersed in operational details. Executives coordinate activities by funding all the products and services from various groups required to execute a strategy. There's no need to intervene in each manager's priorities.

Furthermore, they have better information to decide enterprise priorities. For example:

*   For existing product lines, executives have the information they need to judge product-line profitability and the availability of funds for growth initiatives such as marketing programs, product innovation, and internal process improvements.

*   For new strategies, executives have a realistic view of the total cost of proposed initiatives — not just the obvious direct costs, but their impacts enterprisewide.

---

*I've led an organization using internal market economics,
and another that implemented so-called "best practices."
The one using market economics took half the management effort,
and was much more responsive to changes in its external environment.*

John P. Gillispie
Executive Director - MOREnet
and former CIO, State of Iowa

As an added benefit, trust (and investor confidence) is built through financial transparency before the fact, not just after results are reported.

Bottom Line

When an organization grows beyond a small, tightly knit team, it must find its way around the executive bottleneck.

It takes more than the right talent, whether that's developed internally or brought in from outside.

It takes more than mentoring, whether provided by the board of directors or a professional coach.

Growing organizations need disciplined processes to empower leaders without loss of control; to develop information for effective decision making; and to offer financial transparency.

Internal market economics controls resources and coordinates activities without unproductive bureaucracy. Just the opposite, it encourages customer focus, entrepreneurship, individual accountability, teamwork, and innovation at every level of management.

With both control and coordination in place, top executives no longer need to be immersed in the details. They can empower staff, and move into the role of coaches rather than controlling bosses. This gives them more time to focus on the important issues: strategies, relationships, talent, organization, vision, and inspiration — on growing the top line while investing the scarce resources that those revenues produce.

Internal market economics effectively controls and coordinates organizations of any size. It will support growth indefinitely — an investment that pays off for years to come. It's a practical, straightforward, and effective way to evolve a founder-led firm or rapidly growing internal service provider into a mature, empowered organization with unlimited potential.

17. Summary of Differences

The impacts of internal market economics are profound. Here's a quick summary of the changes it induces:

From: The organization chart is defined in vague terms of roles, responsibilities, functions, and processes.

   To: Every group is an entrepreneurship, with a clearly defined product line.

From: Managers defend their budgets by justifying their costs. They may build in "fat" knowing they'll be asked to cut.

   To: Managers propose budgets for the true, full cost of all the products and services they might sell. Customers decide which they'll buy, and defend the budget for these products and services.

From: Budget decisions are based on past years' spending, the costs of existing staff, and proposed expenditures.

   To: Budget decisions fund well-defined products and services which are selected based on business needs, payoff, and strategic relevance.

From: Strategy decisions are based on rough estimates of the obvious direct costs.

   To: The full cost of a strategy can be calculated by adding up the costs of all the individual products and services required from every organization in the enterprise.

From: Strategic alignment is accomplished through written plans, with the expectation that managers will read the plans and translate enterprise strategies into individual performance objectives.

To: Strategic alignment is accomplished by funding all the products and services enterprisewide that add up to successful execution.

From: Funding for enterprise-good services (Subsidies) is imbedded in clients' deliverables and makes internal service providers look uncompetitive, while making these services appear free and demand for them unchecked.

To: Funding for enterprise-good services is provided through direct budget, and is explicitly decided based on the cost and value of each service.

From: Funding for infrastructure and innovation (Ventures) is controversial and unpredictable.

To: Basic sustainable innovation is built into rates. Funding for infrastructure and other significant investments is provided through direct budget, decided by enterprise executives rather than by clients.

From: The deliverables expected for a given level of budget are unclear; and clients blame internal service providers if their resources are insufficient to satisfy all clients' requests.

To: Clients understand exactly what's funded in an internal service provider's budget; and if they want more, all they have to do is provide the necessary incremental funding.

From: Internal service providers attempt to control their total costs by judging and filtering clients' requests.

    To: Internal service providers are accountable for competitive rates, but clients must manage demand to control total costs.

From: "Governance" means bureaucratic hurdles and steering committees that micro-manage internal service providers.

    To: "Governance" means a portfolio-management process wherein clients manage checkbooks and buy what they most need, adjusting priorities dynamically throughout the year.

From: Chargebacks are a way to spread internal service providers' costs to business units, even though business units can't control them.

    To: Chargebacks empower clients to choose what they buy from internal service providers, and give clients meaningful control of their costs.

From: Teamwork is based on loosely defined roles, interpersonal relationships, and good-will.

    To: Teamwork is based on internal customer-supplier relationships; groups subcontract with peers to buy clearly defined deliverables.

From: Managers are measured on actual spending versus planned.

    To: Managers are measured on the net of revenues minus expenses (break-even or profit targets), and are free to grow their businesses to meet funded demand.

From: Entire organizations may be outsourced if their total costs appear high in comparison to vaguely defined, high-level benchmarks.

To: Every entrepreneur "buys" instead of "makes" if it's more economical to do so — strategic sourcing — utilizing vendors wherever, and only where, they really offer better value.

From: Cost cutting squeezes every manager's budget; and with managers independently deciding what slips, the entire organization becomes less capable of delivering anything.

To: Cost cutting starts with trimming deliverables. Then, managers eliminate the costs of those deliverables, leaving remaining projects and services fully funded.

From: Metrics are limited to annual performance reviews.

To: In addition to performance reviews, managers are measured objectively based on whether they deliver the products and services they promised at a competitive price, and on whether their customers are satisfied with them.

From: Executives personally coordinate and control the activities of the organization.

To: Managers are empowered, and economic processes control their spending and coordinate their activities. Executives provide direction by deciding which initiatives to fund.

THE BENEFITS

18. Financial Benefits

If you're already sold on the merits of internal market economics and you're prepared to convince others of the value of implementing these concepts, then you may wish to skip to Chapter 21 and explore the components of design and implementation.

But be forewarned: Like any meaningful transformational change, it takes an investment of time, thought, and money to implement internal market economics. This and the following two chapters explore the benefits, both to help you make that investment decision and to help you convince others of your decision.

Internal market economics contributes to shareholder value in many ways.

> *Note for not-for-profit and government organizations:* The term "shareholder value" applies to you as well, although it can't be taken literally. It means contributions to the mission of the enterprise, and to the well-being of stakeholders such as the beneficiaries of charities and the taxpayers who fund governments.

The obvious benefits are financial. Resource decisions are better informed — both budget decisions and decisions made throughout the year. Therefore, leaders make wiser choices. They find cost savings, and they choose investments with better returns.

This chapter enumerates those financial benefits. The following two chapters describe the improvements in relationships between internal customers and suppliers, and the transformational benefits — impacts on an organization's culture, structure, teamwork processes, and leadership.

Cost Savings, Level One — External Costs

In market economics, managers succeed by offering the best deal. They are incented to drive their costs down so as to compare favorably with outsourcing, and so that their customers will buy more because their products and services are a good value.

Managers are frugal in many ways:

*   When managers develop budget proposals, there's little incentive to build in "fat" (exaggerate costs). Making yourself look more expensive only induces your internal customers to buy less, or to look elsewhere.

*   Managers include only costs that are necessary to produce their products and services, since all costs must be associated with their proposed deliverables.

*   Headcount is an *output* of the plan, not an input. Staff-hours required to produce each deliverable are calculated, without presuming that current headcount will be appropriate. This reality is a double-edged sword: Managers don't have to promise more work with the same headcount; and if the workload doesn't justify current headcount, then people will have to be redeployed.

*   Managers consciously plan their unbillable time. Hours are set aside for necessary (but indirect) sustenance activities such as professional development, process improvements, administration, customer relationship building, etc.

*   They are careful about vendor costs (the things they purchase to equip and sustain their groups). Indirect costs are planned within the context of their demand forecasts.

*   They choose "buy" over "make," utilizing vendors instead of staff whenever it's more economical to do so (strategic sourcing).

*   There's no incentive to spend all one's budget before year-end in order to get the same budget next year. Last year's spending and current headcount have little relevance (other than the use of historic trends to forecast some future costs).

In each of these ways, managers are frugal but not penurious. They're careful to not waste money, but they don't jeopardize their ability to deliver promised products and services. They cut costs, but they don't cut any corners that shouldn't be cut.

We found some significant savings.
Some of it we would have done anyway, but the
exercise of building a detailed inventory of products and services
revealed several opportunities to [save money].

Keith Wyrick
Director, Finance and HR Applications
Sonoco Products Company [31]

Of course, internal market economics only reveals costs savings if money was being wasted in the past. So the amount cannot be predicted. But most organizations experience savings that more than justify the investment in internal market economics.

Beyond the initial year, internal market economics creates ongoing incentives for frugality.

Cost Savings, Level Two — Internal Costs

Internal support services — products and services that managers buy from peers within the same organization — often represent a significant portion of an organization's cost structure. Traditionally, support groups' budgets are managed in total; but their specific deliverables are rarely scrutinized.

In investment-based budgeting, all support services are treated as products and services, and are scrutinized for value. Internal customers decide what they buy, knowing that the cost of these support services will go into their rates.

Like level one, managers cut costs wherever the value of internal support services is marginal. But they don't eliminate the services they need, and may even buy additional services that make their groups more productive and effective.

Again, internal market economics cuts costs in just the right places.

Cost Savings, Level Three — Demand Management

Once an internal service provider is as lean and efficient as it can be (levels one and two) and compares favorably with its competitors such as outsourcing and decentralization, the only remaining opportunity for cost-cutting is demand management.

Budgeting is zero-based. Rather than arbitrary targets (like prior years' budgets plus or minus a few percent) or industry averages (like functions' costs as a percentage of corporate revenues), each deliverable is decided on its merits. "Keep the lights on" operational deliverables are scrutinized as well as new initiatives.

When clients learn the full cost, they may voluntarily withdraw requests that they don't feel comfortable defending. And pursers spend their precious money on only the best investments, and cut costs by forgoing marginal deliverables.

As a result, "There's a pretty tight link between business requirements and required IT infrastructure," said Steve Wyatt, head of IT infrastructure at Sonoco Products Company. "Upper management within the customer base now knows that their costs are directly proportional to the services they consume."

Executives also explicitly examine "enterprise-good" services such as policy formulation, safety and security, and community citizenship. Rather than leaving these costs haphazardly buried in everybody's budgets, they see the cost of these initiatives and evaluate each on its merits. This makes an enterprise more judicious in its demands for these resource-consuming activities. Again, only the really worthwhile services are funded.

This demand-management process is not limited to the budget cycle. The need for a budget cut may occur mid-year. If it does, the portfolio-management process portrays the cuts as a reduction in the clients' checkbooks. Pursers must decide which products and services they'll do without. Then, the full cost of eliminated deliverables can be removed, while the fewer things the enterprise must continue to do remain fully funded.

Managing costs through demand management discourages projects with poor or negative returns. Just as important, it ensures that projects with the highest returns get done.

Optimal Allocation of Scarce Resources

The optimal level of budget for an organization has little to do with last year's budget plus or minus a few percent. It's based on the investment opportunities at hand.

Investment-based budgeting documents the costs of proposed deliverables. This equips executives to fund well-defined products and services which are selected based on the needs of the business, returns on investments, and strategic investment opportunities.

Dr. Joyce Mitchell, CIO and associate dean at the University of Missouri Health Services, offers an example. [32]

"We have literally hundreds of projects and services that we deliver to keep things running well and to track patients, students, and treatments," she said. "If we didn't get our projects funded properly, the hospital would be chaos.

"But when I added the number of people I needed for these projects to what I needed just to keep the place going, it was a large budget. Senior management said, 'We're just going to give you last year's budget.' And I said, 'Then I can't afford to do anything new.'"

Having implemented investment-based budgeting, Mitchell had the facts to prove her assertion. Executives recognized that the projects which would have to be sacrificed were not optional. "My budget has probably doubled," Mitchell reports.

With investment-based budgeting, worthwhile deliverables (those with good ROI and strategic relevance) are funded, and no more.

Customers Defend Internal Service Providers' Budgets

Aside from Subsidies and Ventures, there's never a need for an organization to sponsor its own projects. Internal service providers may proactively help clients discover new opportunities. But investment-based budgeting makes it clear that every project and service-level agreement must have a specific customer.

It's equally clear that if the client isn't interested in justifying the cost, the deliverable can be dropped and budgets reduced.

As a result, clients naturally step forward and defend the funding for projects and services that benefit them.

And they're highly effective at doing so. With their superior knowledge of their business strategies and how internal service providers' products and services will help them achieve their objectives, clients make a strong case.

This adds to executives' insights, so that budget decisions are based on a deeper understanding of the value of internal service providers' products and services.

As an interesting side effect, when clients defend the budget for internal service providers, the result may be an increase in funding, even in difficult years.

Lew Davison, CIO at the Missouri Department of Transportation (MODoT), was an early pioneer in investment-based budgeting. [33] He first submitted a budget for his organization's products and services in 1999, a year when tax revenues were down. Initially he was expected to cut his budget by seven percent, as were all the other executives. But this time, things turned out differently.

Davison explained, "Clients took an active role in defending their particular projects," he reported. This allowed executives to verify that clients cared enough to fight for the projects they wanted. Plus, client involvement gave executives better information about the benefits of projects, and improved the odds that key projects got funded.

"Without [investment-based budgeting], management would not have known about the specific opportunities that would deliver high ROI. Our budget, I'm sure, would have been slashed with the rest of them. But with [investment-based budgeting], we were able to present opportunities, and we clearly showed that an across-the-board cut wouldn't work," said Davison.

Clients argued that they needed more IT to save money building roads. As a result, while the rest of the budgets in MODoT were shrinking, Davison's IT budget actually went up ten percent.

My organization had been under-spending on information technology for years. With [investment-based budgeting], at a time when other budgets were shrinking, my budget actually went up because clients were able to defend their worthwhile investments.

Lew Davison
CIO
Missouri Department of Transportation

Whether the total budget goes up or down, engaging clients in defending the internal products and services they need results in better budget decisions.

Informed Strategy Decisions

In the business-within-a-business paradigm, one group is the "prime contractor" (project or service-delivery manager) for a given enterprise initiative. That prime contractor buys from other organizations any needed components and support services. Those subcontractors (team members) may, in turn, buy what they need from others.

Thus, every enterprise initiative (or ongoing operational process) engages organizations throughout the enterprise in an internal "value chain." [34]

When every organization in an enterprise prepares an investment-based budget, all the contributors to an enterprise strategy are visible, and the costs of their respective contributions are known. Adding them up shows the total enterprisewide cost of the initiative.

A view of full cost may show that seemingly attractive strategies are not worthwhile, while other strategies (perhaps less costly or less glamorous) may demonstrate higher-than-expected returns.

Similar to evaluating strategies, this enterprisewide view of costs is fundamental to understanding the profitability of existing product lines, markets, acquisitions, and entire lines of business. It allows executives to identify unprofitable activities, and either improve or discontinue them, just as it helps them make the right investments in new opportunities.

Strategy Execution

Another important outcome of enterprisewide investment-based budgeting is improved strategy delivery. Executives not only see the cost of entire strategies — they fund all the products and services enterprisewide that add up to successful execution.

Thus, if a strategic initiative is approved, every participating organization (the "prime" and each of the internal subcontractors) is committed to specific deliverables, and has the resources it needs to deliver them successfully. This is far better than deciding budgets organization by organization, with no explicit process for ensuring that all the pieces of an enterprise strategy are funded.

For example, when Minnesota-based St. Mary's Hospital merged with the Duluth Clinic, their challenges included setting up a common infrastructure for the medical clinics and hospitals, and integrating enterprisewide operations such as patient scheduling, registration, and records. This led to a tremendous demand for information systems.

Robert Bender, CIO of the merged SMDC Health System, said, "When we started the budgeting this year, senior management said, 'Here's the target. Here's what to set your budget at for this next fiscal year.'" But, as he explained, "The demand was virtually infinite, and we were expected to be able to respond. Period." [35]

Investment-based budgeting was a key step in Bender's comprehensive organizational design program. "No question about it, the perception was that IT resources were free. So we went back and listed all of the things we could and couldn't do based on the target. Then we told the senior executives the things our internal customers wanted that couldn't be done."

On that "couldn't be done" list were projects that were essential to integrating the two companies. "As a result, we had over half a million dollars put back into the IT budget," Bender reported.

Of course, the point is not winning a bigger budget. SMDC provided sufficient funding to IT once it saw the link between costs and its top strategic initiative. Had they not done so, their most important strategy would have been at risk.

Further aiding strategy execution, individual accountabilities are absolutely clear. Beyond just the vague language of plans, each manager signs up to deliver well-defined results — specific products and services. This is much more explicit than depending on individual managers to interpret (guess) how they might contribute to published strategic plans, where the language is often vague and priorities are described at a high level.

Investment-based budgeting improves strategy execution by driving specific accountabilities down to individual managerial groups, and providing each with the resources it needs for successful delivery.

Portfolio Management

Internal market economics empowers clients, represented by pursers, to choose which specific projects and services they'll buy from internal service providers. Clients know their needs and the value of internal services to their businesses, so they're in the best position to decide. This aligns internal service providers with the needs of the businesses they serve, virtually automatically.

Bernie Campbell, CIO at Sonoco Products Company, gave an example of clients making better decisions about what they buy, once they have the right information: "[Our investment-based budget] helped divisions which historically spent a high proportion of their IT budget on minor enhancements to legacy systems to realize that they could shift dollars to higher payback new applications by freezing those legacy apps. We never had the facts to present to our clients before." [36]

Pursers manage checkbooks and adjust priorities throughout the year. When pursers change what they buy, the flow of funding to managers changes, causing them to adjust their priorities. As internal "prime contractors" adjust their own priorities, they adjust what they buy from their internal suppliers. Thus, business priorities ripple through the entire internal supply chain, keeping everybody's priorities aligned with ever-changing business needs throughout the year.

This makes internal service providers flexible and responsive, and ensures that scarce resources are continually channeled to the places they're most needed, dynamically maximizing returns throughout the year.

This business-driven resource-governance process involves more than an "executive steering committee" that sets priorities. Pursers know how much is in their checkbooks and how much each of the provider's products and services costs. Unlike simple priority-setting processes (i.e., rank-ordering projects), pursers can examine trade-offs and optimize the overall returns on their checkbooks — true investment portfolio management.

Reliable Delivery

There are certainly costs to an enterprise if organizations within it cannot reliably deliver all their commitments. When internal service providers disappoint their customers, business initiatives are jeopardized.

Internal market economics addresses some of the most critical ingredients of reliable delivery:

*   An investment-based budget describes the full cost of proposed products and services. There's no place for the "do more with less" demand, which forces you to promise more than you have resources to deliver. Instead, the enterprise funds the few things it chooses to buy, and does without the rest. Thus, approved projects and services are fully funded, and no group should lack the resources it needs to deliver on every commitment.

*   Entire project/service-delivery teams are funded — the prime contractor and all internal subcontractors. This ensures that no project fails for lack of support from every member of the team.

*   Individual accountabilities are clear. Within teams, everybody's deliverables are defined, and the chain of command (from the prime contractor to subcontractors, and to their subcontractors) is clear.

*   Costs include appropriate levels of funding for critical sustenance activities. Tasks like professional development, innovation, customer relationship-building, proposal writing,

process improvements, and administration are built into rates. Thus, there's no need to sacrifice these internal investments which are critical to delivery, now and in the future.

* Internal support functions within an organization are adequately funded and grow in proportion to the growth of the business, since these indirect costs are built into the rates for all products and services sold to clients. Thus, everybody is more reliable and productive because they get the support services they need.

* Funding for infrastructure, innovation, and major process improvements (Ventures) is explicit — distinct deliverables decided during the budget process.

* New demands which arise during the year are also fully funded. Internal service providers get incremental revenues sufficient to cover all their costs without impinging on other projects and services. There should never be a need to "rob Peter to pay Paul."

Improved reliability ripples throughout an enterprise. When an internal service provider is reliable, its customers are no longer surprised and disappointed by a failure to meet their expectations. Thus, they too become more reliable.

Basis for External Pricing

Knowing the true, full cost of products and services can help set external prices.

In some government contractors and regulated utilities, revenues are set to cost plus a percentage markup. Here, knowing the full cost of all products and services is essential to external pricing.

Even if pricing isn't cost based, knowing the full cost of your products and services before setting external rates ensures that you don't inadvertently lose money.

Additionally, some internal service providers bring in external business ("in-sourcing"). Aside from the profits (which generally aren't material in the greater scheme of things), there are benefits to the enterprise of these external sales:

* Growth saves money through economies of scale.

* A larger organization can afford a higher degree of specialization, which means better quality, faster innovation, lower costs of learning curves, faster time to market, etc.

* External competition forces internal service providers to treat clients as customers, and to offer the best value. It drives results like:

    - A relevant catalog of products and services
    - Investment-based budgeting
    - An account-representative function
    - Proposal writing (with alternatives)
    - Contracting
    - Time and infrastructure-utilization tracking
    - Invoicing for work delivered
    - Benchmarking rates against external vendors
    - A culture that's customer focused, entrepreneurial, team-oriented, and accepts individual accountability

All these things benefit internal clients.

There are two conditions which must be satisfied before external sales are permissible:

1) Never make counter-strategic sales, such as to a direct competitor of the enterprise.

2) Never impinge on your ability to serve internal customers.

To satisfy condition 2, you have to know the full cost of your products and services (and, of course, charge external customers at least that). Otherwise, external sales may burden indirect support functions, and reduce your ability to serve internal clients. Product/service costing provides this, enabling external sales.

Basis for Profitability Analysis

The costs of specific support services are assigned to the business units that utilize them in a way that's far more accurate than high-level allocation formulas. This makes visible the real, full costs of running each business unit.

Accurate profitability metrics help executives manage business units. They also help with planning, for example, anticipating the costs of growth.

Beyond accuracy, there's the issue of fairness. Since cost allocations generally aren't controllable, it's unfair and unproductive to use allocations to incorporate internal service providers' costs in business units' metrics. But an internal market economy gives each business unit the authority to choose what it buys from internal services providers. With that authority comes accountability for the costs of their purchase decisions.

Profitability analysis can be taken all the way through to the product-line level if externally-facing business units build their own cost models, applying the costs of internal support functions to specific external product lines. This gives an accurate picture of the real, ongoing costs of sustaining each product line.

Bottom Line: Shareholder Value

From a purely financial point of view, the benefits come down to four things:

*   Costs are tightly controlled.

*   Scare resources are channeled to the highest-return uses.

*   Products and services are delivered reliably and efficiently.

*   Accurate pricing and profitability analyses prevent inadvertent losses, and improve executive decision making.

These effects are not just short-term; they're lasting. Internal market economics establishes processes that continually manage costs, continually align resources with ever-evolving business strategies, continually maintain viable businesses within the business, and continually enable reliable service delivery.

19. Relationship Benefits

The benefits of internal market economics go far beyond the financial. It enhances relationships between internal customers and suppliers. And it has transformational impacts (discussed in the next chapter).

This chapter looks at how relationships between internal service providers and their clients are improved. In addition to reduced stress, better relationships have tangible benefits to the enterprise.

Trust Through Transparency

When J.L. Albert took on the job of CIO at Georgia State University in 2005, relationships with clients were strained. "They saw us as a budgetary black hole," he said. "They didn't trust us, and honestly believed we were inefficient and should have been giving them a lot more services." [37]

It got so bad that the Faculty Senate formed a committee to investigate Albert's department, Information Systems & Technologies (IS&T), believing that they'd save money if IT were decentralized. "They thought they were going to pore through my books and find big stashes of money that we'd been hiding!" Albert laughed.

One of Albert's early leadership initiatives was the implementation of investment-based budgeting. He presented the results to the faculty committee, showing them what they got for their fee-for-service payments, as well as all the services they received "for free" which were funded by his direct budget.

As James Amann, business planning coordinator in IS&T, said, "We walked in with a stack of reports this big, and said, 'What else do you want to know?' The conversation shifted extremely rapidly from, 'What's IS&T doing with all that money?' to, 'Where is the *decentralized* IT spending going?'" [38]

Albert challenged the faculty to provide the same visibility into the costs of their local IT groups. As a result, instead of accusing IS&T of costing too much and advocating more decentralization, the faculty committee began investigating potential savings through consolidation of duplicate IT services.

There's nothing like having the data at your fingertips.
We can counter every ill-founded protestation with hard facts.

James Amann
Business Planning Coordinator
Information Systems & Technologies
Georgia State University [39]

Amann said, "We can present our budget to clients in whatever level of detail they want. If they want it, we can dive down to every single dollar."

Clients see why things cost what they do, and what internal service providers are doing with the funding they get. They realize that internal service providers are not wasting, or hiding, money. And they understand that all funding ultimately benefits them.

"Now, there's a new level of trust," Albert continued, "because I've got more reliable numbers than they've got about their own [decentralized] IT spending."

Doug Volesky, assistant administrator in the Information

Technology Services Division (ITSD) at the State of Montana, provided another case example. The State had been squeezing ITSD's budget for years, to the point where it couldn't be a reliable service provider.

After implementing investment-based budgeting, Volesky said, "Transparency is a huge thing. Almost all the agencies didn't get any increase whatsoever; and we got about a $3 million increase that wasn't even questioned." [40]

Volesky would be the first to point out that it's not about getting more money; it's about building trust in your numbers to get what you need to meet your commitments.

In addition to transparency, rates are comparable to vendors' prices. Like-for-like benchmarks often prove that internal service providers offer the best deal. This, too, enhances trust.

Perception of Value Received

Internal market economics helps clients understand the value they receive from internal service providers.

An investment-based budget describes exactly which products and services are to be delivered for a given level of funding. Beyond just a product/service catalog, it produces a clear, understandable list of all specific products and services to be expected for a given level of funding.

Thus, clients know exactly what they're getting for their money.

"I can give you an example," Albert said. "One of the colleges always thought they were overpaying when they wrote IS&T a check for $200,000 per year. I was able to show them that they were actually getting $1.4 million worth of services, most of which was paid by the university IT budget. All of a sudden, someone who had been an adversary became my advocate! They started defending my budget."

[Investment-based budgeting] allowed us to deflate large buckets of general cost and appropriate the costs to those departments that were actually using the services ... initiating some substantial discussions around the value we bring to each of those business units.

David Caldwell
Director, IT
Compassion International

Then, throughout the year, internal market economics reinforces clients' understanding of value they're getting through invoices which itemize the specific products and services that were delivered, and the costs associated with each.

Changes the Dialog

Internal market economics changes the dialog between internal service providers and their clients. Instead of saying something to the effect of:

"I need headcount; here's why...."

...managers say:

"Here are my proposed products and services, and their costs. I'm happy to explain where the numbers came from (transparency) and compare my rates to alternatives like outsourcing (benchmarks).

> *"Once you've validated that I'm a good deal, let's take a look at what your people want from me — proposed projects and services. What are you willing to buy?"*

All costs are linked to products and services, and subject to scrutiny first by the organization's executive, and then by auditors and clients. After the cost model is validated, discussion returns to the deliverables and a rational analysis of the value to the business of proposed projects and services.

Dialog shifts from "Why do you cost so much?" to "What products and services do we need from you, and how can they contribute to our strategies?"

Sure, changes in the costs of ongoing services from year to year have to be explained, and rates may periodically have to be benchmarked. But once trust is built (e.g., by benchmarking rates), discussions become simple, businesslike, and not at all bureaucratic or political.

Keith Wyrick, director of finance and HR applications and a key client liaison at Sonoco Products Company, shared their experience. [41]

"[In the past] we spent many hours on a fundamentally flawed process. We would try to come up with a reasonable estimate of next year's expenses based on current spending. We'd add or subtract from that based on expectations for either growth (new projects) or contraction (retired applications, closed plants, etc.). This would take several weeks, even months. If the submitted budget was too high, we had to go back to the drawing board."

Wyrick explained that they would attempt to negotiate service levels with clients. "We'd demonstrate how the addition of five new applications would require additional support. But if the cost exceeded last year's budget, they'd say these applications were different and wouldn't really require support! We used historical billing records to try to justify our numbers. But this had limited success."

As much as they wanted to help clients understand the impacts of budget decisions on service levels, "by then, we'd run out of time; so instead of figuring out which services to cut, we would just take a proportional amount from each line item and resubmit it."

This produced budgets that were out of synch with the growing needs of the business, and IT staff without sufficient resources to meet clients' burgeoning expectations. As Wyrick said, "If it took 200 hours to support an application this year, you can't expect to budget 200 hours next year AND promise enhancements AND an upgrade."

After implementing investment-based budgeting, Wyrick told a different story.

"Our budget presentations to the business units were supported with a lot of detail; [they] were more fact based. [As a result] our conversations changed. Instead of general discussions, we went through each deliverable and how this year's actuals would translate into next year's budget. For the first time, there was virtually no debate. The facts are disarming. We had a number of meetings to explain the details, but that was it."

Over time, investment-based budgeting continued to enhance relationships with clients. "It took a lot of the stress out of the process," Wyrick observed. "Now, we give them detailed spreadsheets of their [proposed] charges, and our discussions are specific to products, services, and costs."

Jackie Ponder, Sonoco IT's budget manager, added, "One benefit that I see is that we get fewer questions about our costs from our customers, and have more meaningful discussions of business needs."

The facts are disarming.

Keith Wyrick
Director of Finance and HR Applications
Sonoco Products Company [42]

Customers Control Their Purchase Decisions

Clients are empowered to decide what they will and won't buy, both during the budget negotiation process and throughout the year. This is true even if clients pay allocations or if an internal service provider receives its funding through a direct budget.

This entire process is businesslike and straightforward.

Clients submit requests for funding to their pursers, and supply whatever information their pursers may require. Business-unit pursers have every right to demand justifications. But this is common sense, not bureaucracy. Forms, scorecards, policies, and hurdle rates of return are replaced with an explanation to pursers of the business needs and the expected benefits.

Even if an internal service provider has been granted a monopoly in some or all of its lines of business, clients are in control. A monopoly doesn't allow clients to spend their checkbooks elsewhere; but at least they decide what checks to write.

The business leaders understood each of our deliverables — what, when, and how much — and felt in control of what they bought from us. IT became more of a partner and less of a constraint in their business planning.

Bernie Campbell
CIO
Sonoco Products Company

Being in the driver's seat eliminates the resentment that arises when internal service providers decide their own priorities, and then internal customers have to beg suppliers to fulfill their requests. With internal market economics, the frustration with bureaucratic demand-management processes fades.

Allocations Under Client Control

If an internal service provider allocates its costs to the business, clients naturally resent "taxation without representation."

But in an internal market economy, allocations (if any) are not a way to spread an organization's costs to its clients. Instead, they create checkbooks (prepaid accounts), and clients decide what checks to write to purchase an internal service provider's products and services.

When clients understand that they're in control of their allocations, resentment wanes. Allocations become nothing more than a reasonable way to make spending more predictable.

Furthermore, clients stop complaining about the size of their allocations when they see exactly what they're getting for their money — the list of specific projects and service-level agreements that are funded by their allocations.

It also provides a factual basis for setting allocation levels. Amounts can be determined by summing the costs of the deliverables for each business unit which were approved in the budget process. Thus, allocations are fair (based on consumption), and clients can influence the amount of their allocations through their involvement in the budget process.

If a business unit wants to reduce its allocation, it's free to do so; but it'll have to decide what it will *not* buy from the internal service provider.

On the other hand, if it wants more (as clients inevitably do), it'll have to pay more. In this case, a business unit must either submit a larger allocation so that it has a bigger checkbook to spend on the internal service provider, or it will have to provide additional fee-for-service funding during the year.

Either way, controversy over the size of allocations disintegrates. In fact, once allocations are linked to the products and services they receive and are treated as checkbooks they own, clients may say: "My allocation is too *small!*"

Managing Expectations

If you don't manage expectations up front, you'll be blamed when you can't deliver all that clients want, or all that you delivered in the past, despite budget cuts — the ludicrous "do more with less" demand.

Volesky recalled their difficulties before Montana's ITSD

implemented investment-based budgeting. "When budgets get tight, the State wants to know what's included in [our budget and] rates, and we have a hard time explaining what's all in there. [43]

"They also tell us, 'It's too high; you need to cut 10 or 15 percent off your total budget.' So we do that, but we ...don't have the tools to explain what services will be cut off. We're not able to tell them, 'This is what you're getting.' So they expect a lot more than we're able to provide."

An investment-based budget documents what is (and isn't) funded. Clients can no longer expect unlimited services for a fixed price. Their expectations match available resources.

After implementing investment-based budgeting, Volesky reviewed their proposed budget with each state agency before submitting it to the state's Budget Office. He reported, "There's a lot more communication going on with [clients]. They know what they're getting. And if they want something different, they have to pay for it. I definitely think that helped our credibility."

This positive effect continues throughout the year as pursers decide what to buy with their checkbooks. Because pursers are limited to the checkbook created by your budget or allocations, expectations remain in keeping with resources.

Internal market economics eliminates a lot of stress in relation-ships. Clients stop demanding more than internal service providers can deliver. Internal service providers don't feel pressured to make promises they can't keep. And they're not set up to fail as they would be if expectations exceeded their resources.

Internal market economics is an effective, efficient, flexible, and lasting solution to the "managing expectations" problem.

Not an Obstacle

With client pursers deciding priorities, it's no longer up to you to judge clients' requests, or to try to limit clients' demands to fit your available resources. Thus, you're never in the "villain" role, telling clients they can't have what they want.

If clients want more than was originally planned in your budget, you willingly supply it — at an additional cost. When clients supply additional funding, you expand your capacity (e.g., by hiring contractors and vendors) to satisfy incremental demand. So you never have to be an obstacle. This is far better than turning clients away or promising more than you have resources to deliver.

And rather than decrying suppliers as the obstacle, clients learn that it's their responsibility to pay for the products and services they need.

An example came from a source that would surprise some for its businesslike approach — the headquarters of a large religion. [44]

This not-for-profit used to follow a typical process in which annual budgets were based on the previous year's spending, plus a percentage for inflation or other factors.

Managers were evaluated primarily on whether they stayed within their budgets. So when clients wanted IT's help to launch new initiatives, all the CIO could do was add their requests to his growing queue. IT became a constraint to growth.

A thought-leader within the enterprise, this CIO's investigation of a better approach to budgeting for IT ultimately spawned a project to transform the budgeting process of the entire enterprise.

The enterprise kicked off the implementation of investment-based budgeting in January, 2004. The CIO saw an immediate difference. Business managers began proactively calling him about their plans for the coming year so that he could factor new development costs into his budget. "This year, for the first time, I actually have some new items in my budget that are not based on the last 12 months, but based on things that departments want to do," he said.

Demand wasn't new to IT, but getting the resources to deliver new projects was. Working with the cost model, the CIO concluded that he needed eight additional employees. And he could see precisely which deliverables drove the need.

"I went into the [budget] meeting with a lot of apprehension about defending our charges, but that isn't how the meeting went at all," he said. Not only did managers purchase all the deliverables IT offered, but some found out about services that IT had been providing to other departments and wanted to buy them too. The CIO got the headcount he'd requested.

Once they understand internal market economics, clients see internal service providers as being on "their side of the table," with the only obstacle being their own spending power.

Clear Mutual Commitments

Fundamental to internal market economics is a catalog of products and services published by every internal service provider. It serves as a basis for "contracts" which document agreed deliverables and mutual accountabilities.

Internal contracts minimize misunderstandings of what's expected of both suppliers and customers. When both parties know their accountabilities, projects and services are delivered more reliably.

If things go wrong, contracts reduce finger-pointing and assist in diagnosing the root causes of any delivery problems.

An example comes from a Fortune-100 healthcare products company. The corporate HR department wanted to develop the HR information system with its decentralized IT group. But of course it needed a lot of help from Corporate IT, and the application was to run on computer servers owned by Corporate IT.

That project ran into many difficulties, including a problematic launch. HR began to point fingers at IT. But thanks to clear contracts, IT was able to show that it had fulfilled all its contracts for support and operational services, on time and on budget. The head of HR had to look for the root causes of project troubles within his own organization.

Reduced misunderstandings and clear accountabilities all contribute to healthy, businesslike relationships, and to getting the job done.

Bottom Line: Shareholder Value

The benefits of improved relationships between clients and internal service providers are many. Fewer challenges, disagreements, and misunderstandings save time and money. Better collaboration produces better results. And effective partnerships improve delivery, and may even lead to the discovery of creative, high-payoff investment opportunities.

20. Transformational Effects

In addition to financial and relationship benefits, internal market economics has positive impacts on an organization's culture, structure, teamwork, and leadership. This chapter describes these transformational effects.

While internal market economics is invaluable
for planning and governance, the true sustaining value
comes from the transformation of the management team.

Gary P. Rietz
CIO
Schawk, Inc.

Internal Customer Focus

A culture of customer focus is reinforced in a number of ways.

First and foremost, staff learn that they're in business to produce tangible deliverables for others. Vague assertions like "for the good of the company" are replaced with clearly defined customers — both clients and peers within the organization.

James Amann, planning coordinator for Information Systems & Technologies (IS&T) at Georgia State University, illustrated this. "Our managers thought they sold 'IT support' to the University. With investment-based budgeting, we got more connected to our customers. Every manager defined a catalog of specific products and services, and exactly which customers they sell them to." [45]

Instead of them deciding what's best for the enterprise, IS&T staff now understand that customers decide what to buy, and that they have to please their customers to stay in business.

Furthermore, suppliers never have to judge the merits of customers' requests — the opposite of customer focus — in the course of deciding what goes into their budgets, or in deciding which requests are to be fulfilled throughout the year.

Note on monopolies: A culture of customer focus can be cultivated even when an organization has been granted a monopoly in some or all of its lines of business. Staff should be reminded that a monopoly doesn't guarantee their market share (or their jobs), giving them the right to abuse their customers. Instead, it makes market-share an all-or-nothing proposition. If customers are unhappy, rather than complaining (an early warning that something needs to be fixed), they build resentment until relationships deteriorate to the point that an outsourcing study is initiated or a leader is replaced.

Staff should be reminded that the surest way to lose a monopoly is to behave as a monopolist. Despite a monopoly, internal service providers should focus on earning the position of "vendor of choice" through value, performance, and relationships.

Entrepreneurship

"It's tough to find managers with business acumen," said Ralph Caruso, CIO at the University of Maine. [46]

Caruso went on to say, "I've got good people. They're technically competent, hardworking, good at managing others, and loyal. They just don't have a clue how to run a business."

Most senior managers, even executives, rose through the ranks based on their professional competence. Along the way, they acquired supervisory skills — the ability to manage and motivate others.

But few have actually run businesses. They may know how to manage budgets and read financial statements. But they've never had a chance to develop their entrepreneurial skills.

As a result, they may not be equipped to fulfill leadership duties such as business planning, managing internal investments, and maintaining a competitive business. And they may not be contributing all they might to the strategic thinking of the enterprise.

How can an enterprise cultivate entrepreneurial skills in all its leaders?

Internal market economics helps.

We created an environment in which entrepreneurs can flourish.

James Amann
Business Planning Coordinator
Information Systems & Technologies
Georgia State University [28]

Every manager at every level is treated as a business within a business.

First and foremost, this means accepting accountability for results — delivery of products and services — not just for managing resources and processes. With responsibility for their individual catalogs, managers gain a clear understanding of the lines of business they run and the results (products and services) that they're accountable for.

In many cases, delivery of results requires not only the work of one's own group, but also the assistance of internal subcontractors (other groups within the organization). Entrepreneurs learn to manage their suppliers in order to deliver their own products and services.

Beyond accountability for results, entrepreneurship means running a viable and sustainable business.

Entrepreneurs learn to plan their businesses. They forecast expected sales, and understand what revenues they can count on and what their growth opportunities are. They figure out how they're going to fulfill projected sales, linking their costs to their deliverables.

Entrepreneurs learn to be frugal about their costs, knowing that customers may choose to buy from their competitors (decentralization and outsourcing) if they don't offer good value.

They learn to better manage their businesses with key competitive benchmarks, monitoring their competition for two reasons: to stay ahead, and to "buy" instead of "make" whenever it's more economical to do so.

Entrepreneurs minimize costs to remain competitive; but they also offer a range of up-to-date products and services.

Peter F. Drucker said, "...every product and every activity of a business begins to obsolesce as soon as it is started. Every product, every operation, and every activity in a business should, therefore, be put on trial for its life every two or three years. Each should be considered the way we consider a proposal to go into a new product, a new operation or activity — complete with budget, capital appropriations request, and so on. One question should be asked or each: 'If we were not in this already, would we now go into it?' And if the answer is 'no,' the next question should be: 'How do we get out and how fast?'" [47]

Continual innovation is an essential attribute of effective organizations.

Gifford Pinchot III wrote, "Innovation almost never happens in large organizations without an individual or small group passionately dedicated to making it happen. When such people start up new companies, they are called entrepreneurs. Inside large organizations we call them intrapreneurs." [48]

Innovation is the spark that makes good companies great.
It's not just invention, but a style of corporate behavior
comfortable with new ideas and risk. [49]

"Intrapreneurs" proactively set aside time and money for critical sustenance activities such as professional development, technology experimentation, and process improvements. They propose Ventures when they need one-time funding to develop new products and services, or to implement new processes.

They also proactively look for new ways to serve their customers. They're not afraid to propose new things, knowing that if the enterprise chooses to buy more from them, incremental work comes with incremental funding. They uncover customer needs, develop innovative new products and services, and proactively suggest new deliverables that they think may be worthwhile. And they market their services, building understanding of the value they deliver.

Of course, not all these creative new ideas will be funded. It's up to customers to decide what they will and won't buy. But a big stack of new ideas typically has within it a few gems — high-return investments that otherwise may never have surfaced.

John Grover, manager of computing infrastructure at the University of Maine, provided a great example of entrepreneur-ship. The University's IT function was highly decentralized; the various campuses owned and managed their own computer servers. By offering virtual servers utilizing his centralized infrastructure, Grover could save money and provide a more reliable, secure operating environment — without the campuses losing any degree of control.

He marketed this service by explaining the benefits; and he earned the business, client by client. One campus library, for example, owned several servers that were quite old and due for replacement. Grover sold them a more secure and reliable service for a lower operating costs. As Grover sold more clients on this service, the savings added up. In a matter of months, his initiatives saved over $70,000.

Staff who sell support and overhead services also recognize their peers within the same organization as customers. No function is left out of the culture of customer focus and entrepreneurship.

Internal market economics teaches managers to think like empower-ed entrepreneurs. It shifts the culture from bureaucratic (where managers just manage the resources and processes assigned to them) to entrepreneurial (where managers run businesses within a business).

As much as any technical competencies, this experience prepares managers for the next level of their careers (or quickly filters those who'd rather remain at technical levels).

Empowerment

Empowerment means two things: authorities and accountabilities match; and people are managed by results, not told how to produce those results (the "what," not the "how").

The benefits are many; for example, empowerment unleashes everybody's creativity; allows flexibility in processes without loss of accountability; and enhances staff's motivation and retention.

Empowerment is fundamental to individual accountability. If someone else tells you how to do your job and then you fail, is the fault yours or does the blame go to the one who imposed a process on you? Unless people are fully empowered, they can't be held fully accountable for their results.

The impact on management is also important. There's an old saying: *If it takes two of us to do your job, why do I need you?* Managers don't have to "micro-manage" and tightly control staff who are empowered. Empowered staff leave managers free to do their own jobs — plan their businesses within a business, manage people, and engage in strategic thinking.

However, empowerment must not mean chaos (as discussed in Chapter 16). The resources and actions of an organization still have to be tightly coordinated. So the challenge of empowerment is not eliminating controls, but rather replacing top-down controls with systemic governance.

Market economics does exactly this — it's a powerful mechanism of coordination and control.

Perhaps the most famous economist of all time, Adam Smith, in his foundational book, *The Wealth of Nations,* said: "Every

individual endeavors to employ his capital so that its produce may
be of greatest value. He generally neither intends to promote the
public interest, nor knows how much he is promoting it. He
intends only his own security, only his own gain. And he is in this
led by an invisible hand to promote an end which was no part of
his intention. By pursuing his own interest he frequently promotes
that of society more effectually than when he really intends to
promote it." [51]

As in national economies, internal entrepreneurs are empowered to
run their businesses within a business. And because it's in their
own best interests to satisfy customers and make optimal use of
suppliers, what's best for them is aligned with what's best for the
enterprise. Thus, resources are controlled and actions are coordinated without the need for constant management intervention.

Teamwork

When managers independently set their own priorities, one
manager's highest priority may be another's lowest, and teamwork
suffers. For teamwork to work, priorities have to be set
consistently for the whole organization.

Written plans rarely accomplish this well. The language is vague;
priorities are described at too high a level; and plans aren't
updated continually as priorities shift.

In an internal market economy, teamwork is based on internal
customer-supplier relationships. Just like the general contractor
who sells a house and who subcontracts with an electrician,
plumber, roofer, etc., managers buy clearly defined deliverables
from one another.

Teamwork begins before the year starts. In the investment-based budgeting process, all the managers on each team plan the resources they'll need to produce their projects and services — including not just the prime-contractor group but all the needed subcontractors. This is necessary to add up the full cost of each project or service in the budget.

Then, when it's time to deliver projects, peers don't surprise one another with demands for help at the last minute. Entire projects are funded — including the prime contractor and all internal subcontractors. This avoids the situation where managers don't have the resources to support one another.

The quality of teamwork is also improved when prime contractors and internal subcontractors precisely define their respective deliverables and sub-deliverables. Subcontracting with other groups for specific products and services (instead of just for people) clarifies roles and relationships within teams, defining clear individual accountabilities for each team member.

Note the flexibility inherent in this approach to teamwork. When prime contractors buy just what they need from peers, business processes are generated dynamically, employing just the right people at just the right time within each project team. Rather than wait for executives to assign groups to projects, teams are self forming.

The paradigm of buying what you need from subcontractors also makes clear the chain of command within teams. Disputes over control of projects (or lack of clear accountability for the whole project) are eliminated, and teams become self-managing.

With clear individual accountabilities and adequate resources to support one another, the most common reasons for breakdowns in teamwork are eliminated.

Integrity

"Integrity" refers to the behaviors that inspire trust. Delivering reliably on every commitment is fundamental to integrity.

Two of the greatest threats to staff's ability to deliver reliably are insufficient resources, and insufficient support from other groups. Internal market economics eliminates both these obstacles.

Since funding covers the full cost of products and services, staff have the resources they need (including staff time and money for contractors if necessary) to complete every assignment. And funding covers both the prime contractor and all the necessary internal subcontractors.

Another common reason for unreliability is unclear individual accountabilities. When managers contract to sell their products and services, they clearly define commitments that become the basis of measurable deliverables.

Of course, there may be other reasons why people can't be trusted to deliver their commitments, such as a culture which condones making commitments you can't keep, a lack of competencies, or uncontrollable events. But at least an internal market economy eliminates the most common threats to an organization's integrity.

Clear Structure

The first step in determining a catalog of products and services is to define the lines of business under each manager. To do so, managers adopt a common language for labeling internal lines of business. [52] This often reveals opportunities for improving organizational structure.

Managers may discover that a given line of business is scattered among multiple groups. And they often find that they are responsible for multiple, perhaps conflicting, lines of business.

For example, at a healthcare provider in Minnesota, the IT organization had a computer server that was managed and used by their applications developers. Data center staff knew that if they could manage this server, they could improve security, reliability, and efficiency. But they'd been unable to convince the developers to let go of "their computer."

In the planning process, the applications developers were required to develop a business plan and budget for their little computer-operations function, distinct from their applications engineering line of business. They realized that $100/hour engineers were doing work that $25/hour operators could have been doing, and were doing so without the discipline one expects of an operations group — 24-hours-per-day monitoring, physical and logical security, routine backups, business continuity planning, etc.

This experience convinced them that running their server was indeed an operations function, and they willingly moved it into the data center after the planning process was completed.

Facilitating this small structural adjustment, the business plan clearly documented both the budget and staff involved, and the services that the data center was to sell back to the developers. It was a neat package of resources and accountabilities that made the structural change easy.

It's common to find that the experience of defining lines of business and catalogs within an organization, and determining precisely who sells all the internal support products and services, leads to such structural insights. As a separate leadership initiative, a restructuring may result, consolidating redundancies and better focusing specialists.

---

*We continue to find ways of using [investment-based budgeting]
to better understand and manage our business.
It's made us more efficient and more effective.*

Matt Frymire
CIO
Riverside County, CA

Bottom Line: Shareholder Value

Internal market economics makes sense financially, while contributing to the transformational goals of an organization.

Like the financial benefits, the transformational effects add tangible value. Customer focus and entrepreneurship generate creative new investment opportunities, some of which may produce significant returns. Teamwork and integrity produce results more efficiently and reliably. And clarity in the organizational structure may eliminate redundancies and improve synergies.

Unlike many approaches to changing culture and building teamwork, these positive transformational impacts are largely "free" in that they occur in the course of preparing a budget and managing a business, something people have to do anyway.

Internal market economics goes beyond just effective resource-governance processes; it's the foundation for a high-performing organization that's a great place to work.

THE MECHANICS:

IMPLEMENTATION

21. Two Subsystems, and the Components Within Each

In this and the following two chapters, the concept of an internal market economy is deconstructed into its basic components, and guidelines for implementation are provided.

Two Subsystems

Within an internal market economy, there are two major subsystems: Planning, and Actuals.

"Planning" occurs once a year (or, in some government organizations, every other year). Plans may be updated mid-year, but most decisions made during the planning cycle remain valid for a year.

The "Actuals" subsystem operates continually throughout the year. In its processes, people make the kinds of decisions which are updated day by day, week by week, and month by month; and the Actuals subsystem tracks actual results.

These two subsystems are very different — both in their processes and in the tools required. Each must be designed holistically, to work as a system. But the linkages between the two subsystems are limited, well-defined, and do not require that you design everything all at once.

Therefore, implementation can be broken down into two separate steps, designing and installing one subsystem at a time.

Essential Components, and Where They Fit

There are eleven basic components of internal market economics (listed below). Each component will be described in detail in the next two chapters which delve into the two subsystems. This chapter just explains which of the two subsystems each component belongs in.

(Appendix 5 links all these components in an architecture of systems and processes. Appendix 6 breaks out the benefits of each individual component.)

Catalog of products and services: Planning

The product/service catalog must be done in the Planning subsystem, since it's published prior to the start of each year.

Sure, new products and services may be introduced at any time during the year. Nonetheless, as a key output of the Planning subsystem, the catalog is revised and published with rates, and the rates are generally held stable for the year (as described below).

The catalog becomes the basis for business planning as well as for purchase decisions throughout the year.

Business plan: Planning

A business plan forecasts "sales" in the coming year, and then describes how those sales will be fulfilled. The fulfillment plan is where costs are forecasted. The business plan provides the data needed for budgets and rates.

Cost model: Planning

A cost model associates all costs (including indirect costs) with the sales described in the business plan.

The cost model must be imbedded in the Planning subsystem since it's used to produce both an investment-based budget and rates which are published at the beginning of the year.

Investment-based budget: Planning

Obviously, preparing and negotiating a budget is a key output of planning. Using the cost model, an investment-based budget forecasts the costs of all of the products and services in the sales forecast (the business plan).

Rates (unit costs): Planning

Another output of the cost model is rates associated with each item in the catalog.

Rates are generally published at the beginning of a year; and barring some major change in the business (such as an acquisition, divestiture, or consolidation), rates are held stable throughout the year, even if actual costs fluctuate from month to month and deviate from planned costs.

Stable, published rates are critical. Business units plan their budgets with an understanding of what internal support services will cost. If charges differ from the original quotes, clients may not be able to buy what they planned, and their ability to execute their own business plans may be jeopardized.

That "ripple effect" means that if an internal service provider adjusts its rates, business units also should be allowed to revise their plans. And of course, others depend on them in turn. Ultimately, a rate change in a large internal service provider may trigger an enterprisewide revision of everybody's plans — an expensive and time-consuming process.

Stable rates are also a foundation for an internal service provider's planning.

There are cases where actual costs fluctuate significantly, such as where internal service providers are highly dependent on commodities prices, or where the vendor market is changing quickly (perhaps due to new technologies). Where sensitivity to such fluctuations is known in advance, the internal service provider should have the opportunity to hedge; this allows it to offer stable rates to its clients, while still being measured on its ability to manage costs. But if caught by surprise, a mid-year rate adjustment (and perhaps a revision to the enterprisewide plan) may have to be considered.

To hold rates stable throughout the year, the cost model must account for various planning scenarios:

*   On the downside, you must recoup your indirect (fixed) costs in your worst-case scenario.

*   On the upside, you must set labor rates that allow you to bring in more expensive staff-augmentation contractors as you grow (explained in Appendix 3).

Therefore, to set rates properly, they must be calculated within the context of a business plan that forecasts worst-case and best-case scenarios.

Holding rates stable generally means that internal service providers find themselves with a small variance (a profit or loss) at year end. Variances are due to unplanned changes in costs, or to volume changes that affect the apportionment of indirect costs.

These variances are not a problem that justifies frequent destabilizing rate changes. The variances should be analyzed, and then assigned to the enterprise's general coffers.

Assigning variances to clients, as would a co-operative (like a farmers' co-op), is not advisable. It just creates an incentive for clients to micro-manage suppliers' costs so as to get an unearned, profit-enhancing rebate at the end of the year. It distorts business-unit profitability, assigning them variances they cannot control. And it adds no value to decision making.

In summary, because rates are published at the beginning of each year and held stable throughout the year, they are calculated as part of the Planning subsystem.

Client purchase decisions (portfolio management): Actuals

During the budget process, clients decide what they *plan* to buy based on information available at that time. But, of course, things change continuously throughout the year. A more dynamic process is needed to continually revise priorities.

Therefore, the Actuals subsystem includes processes whereby clients decide what they'll *actually* buy throughout the year ("portfolio management").

The Planning subsystem (specifically, the budget) fills up check-books. The Actuals subsystem allows pursers to write checks.

Commitment tracking (internal contracts database): Actuals

When clients decide to purchase an organization's products and services, a "contract" is formed. Contracts are tracked in a database to provide a basis for billing, as well as for the management of resources and commitments.

Since contracts are formed throughout the year as purchase decisions are made, commitment tracking is part of the Actuals subsystem.

Utilization tracking: Actuals

An internal service provider must track the products and services which are delivered. Additionally, costs are tracked.

People's time must be captured through timecards. For infrastructure-based services, metrics of utilization are required.

Of course, utilization (all types) is tracked throughout the year in the Actuals subsystem.

Invoicing and revenue accounting: Actuals

Based on utilization tracking data, an invoice is issued. Invoices are necessary whether or not an organization charges fee-for-service.

For revenues received through a direct budget or through allocations (where the checkbook is maintained as a prepaid account on the internal service provider's accounts), invoices are needed to decrement the checkbook.

For fee-for-service revenues, journal entries are initiated to transfer money from clients to internal service providers.

As part of this component, revenues are assigned to managers. Overhead is stripped from Client and Subsidy deliverables to fund overhead services before revenues are credited to managers (since individual managers cannot independently decide whether to fund overhead services).

Checkbook accounting: Actuals

If an internal service provider receives revenues through direct budget or allocations, then a checkbook which belongs to clients exists within its accounts.

The Actuals subsystem must continually maintain and report account spending and balances — just like the checkbook registers that we all maintain at home.

Dashboards for management and clients: Actuals

The final essential component is the reporting that both managers within an internal service provider and clients need to make decisions throughout the year.

Optional Components, and Where They Fit

Essential components are all required to create the market effect. Optional components improve the quality of data and decision making, and offer some additional benefits.

Benchmarking: Actuals

Entrepreneurs perform even better when they're cognizant of their competition. The ideal competitive benchmark is the comparison of internal rates with external vendors' prices.

Benchmarking uses published rates (from the Planning subsystem) rather than actual costs, since spending fluctuates month-to-month. And in reality, clients care about what they're charged (driven by published rates times utilization), not whether the internal service provider is making a profit or loss (based on actual spending).

There's no need to benchmark actual costs by product and service. There are two distinct questions, answered by two different metrics:

* Benchmarking published rates answers the clients' question, "Am I getting a good deal?"

* Investigating losses on a P&L answers managers' question, "Am I performing according to the plan?"

Taken together, these two metrics answer the question, "Is the organization delivering good value?"

Although comparisons utilize rates from the Planning subsystem, benchmarking is an ongoing process of collecting and updating vendor data. Therefore, it's considered part of the Actuals subsystem. Benchmarks become a part of the metrics (dashboards) which managers monitor throughout the year.

Automated order entry (request management): Actuals

For routine, commodity products and services, an internal web store can automate order taking and processing.

ROI analysis (benefits measurement, total cost of ownership): Actuals

As pursers make purchase decisions, their executive judgment can be seasoned with quantitative analysis of the returns on their various investment opportunities. This analysis is done on a case-by-case basis as purchase decisions are made throughout the year.

Product/service profitability analysis: Actuals

For ongoing monitoring of product/service profitability, the cost model (built in the Planning subsystem) can be replicated in the Actuals subsystem (typically within the invoicing system).

With this enhancement, actual costs can be associated with specific products and services (as are revenues). This refinement enables the dynamic measurement of product/service profitability.

Dependent Processes

Once an internal market economy is functioning, other processes (which may already exist) can be tied in and benefit from the data it produces. By doing so, these other processes become more effective, and they may also contribute to the effectiveness of the internal market economy.

An example is asset data and capacity management. The invoicing system uses asset configuration data to link infrastructure utilization to service agreements. Going the other direction, all this data can be mined to better manage capacity.

Another linkage is to procurement systems. Vendor license data can be tied to utilization metrics to identify compliance problems, and to find potential savings in the form of unused licenses.

Another integration might be to cost-management systems and processes. For example, in IT, telecommunications carriers' expenses are scrutinized to find errors, or unused services. When these invoices are tied into the Actuals subsystem, they can be correlated with client contracts and analysis may be further automated.

22. Planning Subsystem: Investment-based Budgeting and Rates

The Planning subsystem comprises all the processes that occur annually (or bi-annually), rather than continually throughout the year. Mid-year updates may occur, but these are not essential to the functioning of an internal economy.

One key to making market economics work is knowing the true, full cost of all an organization's products and services. The Planning subsystem does just that. It links all projected costs to an organization's products and services.

Specifically, the Planning subsystem produces the following tangible results:

* A business plan (an annual operating plan, not a multi-year strategic plan).

* An investment-based budget (total cost of products and services).

* A definition of every group's line of business, and a catalog of its products and services with rates (unit costs).

This chapter explains all the components, the planning process, the required tools, and the benefits of addressing just the Planning subsystem.

Components

There are five essential components of the Planning subsystem:

Catalog of Products and Services

Planning an organization's catalog begins with a definition of every group's lines of business. (A manager may be responsible for more than one line of business.)

Then, catalogs are defined *within each internal line of business*. This is much easier than attempting to define a single catalog for the entire organization. And, it's better. It pinpoints individual managers' accountabilities for catalog items. Plus, it incorporates all the products and services which are sold internally alongside those sold to clients (essential for accurate cost modeling).

There are strict rules that guide the definition of catalog items.

First and foremost, catalog items must describe things customers buy — things customers own or consume, not cost-drivers, tasks and processes, or technical factors of production.

The catalog must be at the right level of granularity — offering meaningful purchase decisions and trade-offs. Despite the attractiveness of simplicity, catalog items must not be high-level bundles that include many separate purchase decisions. Forcing clients to buy the whole bundle (when they may only wish to buy a subset of it) takes away their ability to make meaningful choices and to manage their costs.

While the appropriate level of granularity is essential, you can't define a catalog item for every product model, configuration, or

unique customer requirement. The right level of generality is also
essential to designing a reasonable, useful catalog.

In addition to the detailed "a la carte" list of products and services,
a catalog may include bundles that are commonly bought all at
once. [53]

For each product and service in the catalog, managers craft a brief
description of what their customers will own or consume (not what
goes into making the product or service). Service-level promises
may also be included. (A bill of materials isn't required until
online order processing is implemented.)

Each item in the catalog also has associated with it a "unit of
pricing" that defines how the product or service will be billed —
its price per *what*. Units must be carefully chosen to be understandable, measurable, controllable, and at the right level of bulk
(e.g., a labor rate is per hour, not per minute or year).

Business Plan

Business planning defines what an organization will deliver in the
year ahead, and how it'll produce those deliverables (including
what resources it'll need to do so). It has two sub-components: a
demand forecast, and a definition of the resources required to
fulfill that demand.

Each manager lists expected "sales" of his/her products and
services (the demand forecast). These deliverables constitute the
actual business forecast on which the rest of the plan is built.

Each distinct purchase decision is a separate deliverable.

The list of deliverables includes not only assured business ("keep the lights on"), but also speculative projects and services that customers might choose to fund over and above the base. Deliverables are tagged with a priority, leading to an assured "pessimistic" forecast and an "optimistic" growth scenario.

Deliverables may be continuations of existing services and projects already approved or underway. New deliverables may be generated by clients' requests, or they may be proposed by managers based on their understanding of clients' needs, business strategies, and the capabilities of new technologies.

(In IT, applications portfolio management may be another source of ideas for deliverables.)

Deliverables include Subsidies and Ventures. Venture ideas may be generated by the internal service provider's strategic plan.

In addition to external deliverables, managers propose internal sales to one another and overhead services sold to the entire organization.

When teamwork is required among groups, managers coordinate their deliverables so that each group plans its share of each project and service. This is the first step in project planning (with more detailed project plans done separately).

Next, each manager forecasts staffing (employees and contractors) required to fulfill his/her demand forecast, and the appropriate billable-time ratios for each type of staff.

They also plan vendor costs, both direct and indirect expenses.

All costs are forward looking. Rates set purely on historic data may not cover future costs, and may not include indirect expenses which have been under-funded in the past. This can lead to perpetuation of problems like a lack of sufficient funding for infrastructure, innovation, and critical sustenance activities. Historic data is just one input to managerial planning.

Cost Model

A cost model associates all costs (direct and indirect) with the deliverables in the sales forecast.

Indirect costs (of all types) are applied to the products and services each group sells. This includes the services they'll buy from one another, as well as vendor costs that support multiple deliverables.

Indirect costs may be spread to all the products and services in a group's catalog. Or they may be placed in "cost pools" and assigned to one or more specific products and services in a group's catalog. Each product or service can draw from multiple cost pools, providing a high degree of flexibility in apportioning indirect costs to just the right deliverables.

In a second-generation cost model (see Appendix 4), cost pools are apportioned by each manager, just within his/her group. Inter-group costs are handled by the sale of internal deliverables.

With internal and overhead deliverables apportioned into the cost of external sales, what remains are client, Subsidy, and Venture deliverables, all at full cost.

Since the cost model is imbedded in the Planning subsystem, it can take advantage of both the pessimistic and the optimistic scenarios.

It amortizes indirect ("fixed") costs so as to break even in the pessimistic forecast, and scales them up linearly as the organization grows.

And it uses the optimistic forecast to calculate "headroom" in labor rates, to account for the premium paid to contractors over employees as the organization grows.

(Details of the cost model are discussed in Appendix 3.)

Investment-based Budget

The investment-based budget portrays the full cost of each deliverable. (See Chapter 6.)

That cost includes both direct and indirect expenses, costs of the prime contractor and all subcontractors. It also includes any reimbursables (pass-throughs) such as project-related travel costs.

An investment-based budget includes both expected sales and speculative sales, giving clients the ability to decide what funding they'll support.

It includes not only deliverables to clients, but also Subsidies and Ventures.

Rates (Unit Costs)

Rates are generally calculated separately for each group within an organization. When managers share a line of business, a blended rate may be calculated.

Rates exclude reimbursable costs (pass-throughs).

Some rates include subcontractors; e.g., the cost of some Amazon products includes the cost of shipping. Most rates do not.

Integrated Process

These components are not distinct processes; they are all facets of an integrated annual planning process.

In a business plan, managers forecast what will be delivered in the year ahead, and how it will be produced.

A realistic budget depends on this demand forecast and fulfillment plan. Without this foundation, a budget can be nothing more than a trend based on past years or a wish-list of things on which an organization wants to spend money without linkage to the value created by those costs.

Put simply, you have to know how much you're going to sell in the year ahead, and how you're going to produce those deliverables, before you know how much budget you need. Therefore, business planning and budget planning should be one integrated process.

Of course, a demand forecast begins with the catalog, and anticipates which of those products and services will be sold, to whom, and in what quantities. So the catalog is a key part of this integrated process.

Both an investment-based budget and rates come from the same cost model. Budget and rates are simply two views of the same data. Using the same data and cost model to calculate both an investment-based budget and rates has two major advantages:

First, two separate analyses are a lot of unnecessary work.

Second, it's important to charge rates during the year that add up to the total costs promised in the budget. If rates don't match the

budget, clients may get budget approved to spend on an internal
service provider, and later find that their budget won't buy what
they thought it would.

Because the catalog, business plan, investment-based budget, and
rates are all tightly interrelated, the Planning subsystem is an
integrated process that's implemented all at once. (This process is
described, step by step, in Appendix 7.)

Management Involvement

Business planning is generally the responsibility of an organization's managers. There are four reasons why they should be
personally involved (rather than delegate the work to a planning or
finance support group):

i.   Managers uniquely know their businesses and their customers.

ii. If they don't author the plan, it's hard to hold managers
     accountable for its delivery.

iii. Through the experience, managers learn to think like
     entrepreneurs, and learn how to plan businesses.

iv. In the course of participation, managers may discover creative
     opportunities to contribute value in new ways.

If there are questions about whether it's worth their time, consider
each step of the planning process (Appendix 7), and the value
received from their involvement at that step (i through iv).

Choose one of the following three modes of participation for each step based on the value you seek from the process:

A. Done by planning/finance staff, with some management input:

   (i) Managers contribute some of their knowledge.

B. Drafted by planning/finance staff, then managers review and "sign off":

   (i) Managers contribute their knowledge.

   (ii) Managers can be held accountable for delivery.

C. Managers prepare the plan, with facilitation and help from planning/support staff:

   All four benefits; i.e., a transformational process.

In general, participation has the greatest value in the early steps. If you don't invest in full participation in those early steps, it's difficult for managers to engage to any greater degree in the later steps.

Obviously, the ideal is full participation (mode C) at every step in the process.

Time Investment

Implementing this Planning process for the first time (with the inherent learning curve) requires eight to twelve months, depending on level of detail and the dedication of the management team.

(Before you give up, note that this is remarkably quick for a significant organizational transformation process. And, of course, subsequent years are *much* quicker.)

Generally, participants spend an average of a day or two a week working on the project. Ideally, a management team continually invests this level of effort in leadership, whether it's this process or other planning and transformational initiatives.

The project manager (perhaps a planning director) typically spends at least half time throughout the process, and full time in the last few months of preparation and during the negotiation process.

This is a lot of time, but it's more than just an investment in the mechanics and the numbers. The length of time is driven by managers' learning curves, and the shift in paradigm — to the business-within-a-business organization — that occurs through the process. Organizations which are already entrepreneurial may find the process easier and move through it more quickly.

Doug Volesky, of Montana's ITSD, offered this experience: "No matter where you go and what you do, you're only get what you put into it. Some of the managers who were complaining the whole time about how much work it took ... [are now] saying this is one of the best things we ever did." [54]

The other organizations described throughout the book — corporations, state and local governments, universities, and not-for-profit institutions — have all come to the same conclusion.

Of course, once the business model is set up, subsequent years' planning becomes easy. The conversion of the data from last year's plan to next year's plan is relatively straightforward: Some deliverables are deleted; new deliverables are added; and the numbers are revised. With the right tools and methods, this planning process takes no longer than traditional budget processes, and may even take less time.

Tools

Many organizations just use spreadsheets to support their planning. But proper tools can make a big difference in the effectiveness of the process. The experience of the IT department at Sonoco Products Company illustrates this. [55]

"Sure we had budget spreadsheets — lots of them!" laughed Bernie Campbell, CIO.

By 2005, Campbell's corporate IT department had come a long way toward being a customer-focused shared-services provider to Sonoco's business units and headquarters staff. But their budget planning process was time consuming, and did little to build trust or give clients meaningful control of their IT spending.

They had defined their products and services and tried to assign costs to each. But it wasn't easy. "It required several home-grown Excel spreadsheets that were very difficult to change," Campbell recalled.

Steve Wyatt, head of infrastructure engineering and services, manages two-thirds of Sonoco's IT budget. "It was very cumber-some," he concurred, "a complex and tightly linked set of spreadsheets." A change in one file would not always be reflected in all the related spreadsheets, some of which might have already been reviewed with clients.

"Each year required a large amount of rework to update them," Campbell noted.

Beyond that, when they wanted to verify where a budget number had come from, they had to spend lots of time looking back through multiple spreadsheets, in some cases examining the date stamp to determine which was the correct version. "The relationship of the separate pieces to the 'finished product' was almost impossible to manage," Wyatt said.

And when problems arose, what did they do? "Build bigger spreadsheets!" Campbell quipped.

Campbell explained why they acquired a commercial budget method and tool. [56] "I was interested in a comprehensive solution that would cover existing and yet-to-be defined scenarios. The risk was quite low compared to the potential benefits: We had to get some relief!"

With the tool, the process got easier. "I spend far less hands-on time during the budget process than I had in the past," Campbell reported. "In addition to speed, we're using the tool in collaborative working sessions with my direct reports. In the past, budget discussions tended to be a series of one-on-one reviews. Now, group discussions focus on underlying principles and business strategy."

And when IT does get questions about their calculations, "We now spend much less time researching why something costs what it costs," said Jackie Ponder, Sonoco IT's budget manager.

Campbell appreciated the value of this. "We explore different scenarios and react to changes in clients' assumptions much faster than before. For example, in 2009, we were able to produce 13 'official' versions of the budget, and a number of informal ones, from July through January."

Appendix 5 describes how Planning tools differ from Actuals systems, from the ground up. And it overviews the requirements of an effective business planning tool.

Costs and Benefits

The Planning subsystem changes the nature of the budget dialog from defending costs to understanding the needs of the business and strategic investment opportunities. Clients defend internal service providers' budgets. Budgets are based on business requirements (not last year plus or minus a percentage). And everyone leaves the budget process with a clear understanding of what's funded and what's not, and of the value delivered for a given level of funding.

In addition to an investment-based budget, the Planning subsystem produces rates that are transparent and fair, and can be compared fairly to outsourcing.

The costs of the Planning subsystem are primarily in learning a new approach to business and budget planning, and the tool that supports your management team in that process.

Implementing the Planning subsystem alone doesn't fully establish an internal market economy, but it does solve the majority of Robert's problems described in Chapters 3:

* "We're not going to propose anything new."
* "You cost too much (for the value we perceive we get)."
* "You're wasting money."
* "Full cost recovery."
* "You don't need all that training."
* "We know you have some fat in there."
* "Do more with less!"
* "It's your job to defend my project."
* "We really don't know the total cost of this strategy."
* "Last year's budget plus/minus a percentage."

* "My allocation is too big."
* "It's your money; do the best you can with it."
* "You're the bottleneck!"
* "You're unreliable and incompetent."
* "I haven't got time to help on your project team."
* "You're not aligned with business strategies."
* "Cut X percent."
* "We should outsource you."
* "This consolidation process is a fiasco."

And the Planning subsystem delivers a majority of the benefits described in Chapters 18 through 20:

* Financial: Cost Savings, Level One — External Costs
* Financial: Cost Savings, Level Two — Internal Costs
* Financial: Cost Savings, Level Three — Demand Management
* Financial: Optimal Allocation of Scarce Resources
* Financial: Customers Defend Internal Service Providers' Budgets
* Financial: Informed Strategy Decisions
* Financial: Strategy Execution
* Financial: Portfolio Management
* Financial: Reliable Delivery
* Financial: Basis for External Pricing
* Financial: Basis for Profitability Analysis
* Relationship: Trust Through Transparency
* Relationship: Perception of Value Received
* Relationship: Changes the Dialog
* Relationship: Allocations Under Client Control
* Relationship: Managing Expectations
* Relationship: Clear Mutual Commitments
* Transformational: Internal Customer Focus
* Transformational: Entrepreneurship

*   Transformational: Empowerment
*   Transformational: Teamwork
*   Transformational: Integrity
*   Transformational: Clear Structure

The breakout of benefits associated with each component of the Planning subsystem is contained in Appendix 6.

23. Actuals Subsystem:
Client-driven Governance

The Actuals subsystem contains the processes that occur continually, or periodically, throughout the year. In the Actuals subsystem, decisions are made about what an organization will actually produce, and the results are tracked.

These ongoing processes presume that, at the beginning of the year, the organization has produced a catalog of its products and services with rates, and an investment-based budget — the outputs of the Planning subsystem.

There's much more to the Actuals subsystem than just charging clients for the products and services they consume. This chapter explains all the components, the required tools, and the benefits of implementing this subsystem.

Components

There are six essential components of the Actuals subsystem, and four optional components:

Client Purchase Decisions (Portfolio Management)

The key to internal market economics is that clients decide what they'll buy from an internal service provider. This is true whether revenues are channeled to an organization via a direct budget, or through clients' budgets via allocations or fee-for-service charge-backs. (See Chapter 5.)

Where fee-for-service chargebacks exist, the client purchase-decision process occurs entirely within clients' organizations. People who wish to buy products and services from an internal service provider need to either have the money in their budgets to pay for their purchases, or convince those in their organizations who have money to fund their requests. An internal service provider has little influence on these decision processes. (In fact, it's not appropriate for an internal service provider to intervene in clients' decisions about how to spend their money, other than to proactively offer alternatives, share its knowledge, and help clients make wise choices when asked.)

However, when an internal service provider receives a direct budget or allocations, a prepaid account is held within its accounts. Some of this pays for Subsidies and Ventures. The remainder goes into checkbooks that belong to clients. For these checkbooks, the internal service provider must engineer governance processes whereby clients decide what checks to write.

There may be a single checkbook shared by the entire enterprise; or there may be a checkbook for each business unit (as is typically the case where business units submit separate allocations). For each checkbook, a purser (perhaps a committee) is designated to represent beneficiaries.

In collaboration with these pursers, policies and procedures are defined to explain how each checkbook is to be used, how decisions will be made, and how clients go about requesting funding for their needs.

It's the internal service provider's job to communicate the full cost of all its products and services. It's the pursers' jobs to decide what they'll buy and accept accountability for the returns on their investments.

It's also the pursers' jobs to communicate their decisions to their constituents. If they don't, internal service providers may be blamed when pursers decide not to provide their clients with a service.

A portfolio-management tool (much like the one you may use to manage your stock portfolio) helps pursers view the in-process and prospective deliverables, with their costs. A checkbook accounting system is also required. (See below.)

Commitment Tracking (Internal Contracts Database)

Once clients decide to buy something and the internal service provider agrees to deliver it, an internal "contract" is formed.

More than a priority list, an internal contract is a solid commitment by the supplier to deliver the agreed product or service, and by the customer to fulfill any necessary customer accountabilities.

Documenting commitments does not need to be bureaucratic. In fact, it *should not* be bureaucratic. Oral contracts may be considered binding. A simple email that confirms the mutual understanding may be considered a contract. For larger purchases, contracts are typically documented in the form of service-level agreements or project charters.

There are many advantages to tracking all these commitments in an internal contracts database.

A contracts database provides a basis for linking utilization data (such as timecards and infrastructure usage) to products and services which clients have agreed to buy. This is essential for invoicing. (See below.)

A contracts database is also useful to internal service providers. By meticulously tracking the commitments they've made, managers can know when their resources will become available before making any new commitments.

Documenting internal contracts can also avoid misunderstandings up front; and when things go wrong, contracts help executives sort out root causes and accountabilities.

An internal contracts database should be kept as simple as possible to avoid unnecessary administrative costs. Typically, a one-page form is all that's needed. The contract must specify the name of the customer, the name of the supplier, the product or service, customer accountabilities, and due dates. Detailed requirements, project plans, and documentation can be considered supporting documents outside the contracts database.

Policies may be needed to know who is authorized to make commitments on behalf of each managerial group. And with fee-for-service contracts, it's important to know whether the requesting client is authorized to spend money.

Once implemented, no billable work should be done without an authorized contract. All staff need to understand this ("closing the back door").

Utilization Tracking

Tracking the products and services that were actually delivered provides the basis for invoicing.

For labor-based services such as engineering and consulting, this involves time reporting. Staff will have to learn which activities are unbillable (sustenance activities for the benefit of their own groups), and which are billable to customers' contracts. This may require a data feed from the contracts database.

Infrastructure utilization, such as the use of computers and networks in IT, is measured by sensors and tracking systems embedded in the equipment. Systems aggregate this low-level data into total utilization of infrastructure components. An asset-configuration database may be needed to associate utilization of infrastructure components with specific contracts.

Reimbursable expenses are extracted from general-ledger data.

Invoicing and Revenue Accounting

An invoicing system multiplies utilization data by published rates (not actual costs), and then adds reimbursables ("pass-throughs"). Given the use of published rates (from the Planning subsystem), an invoicing system does not require an imbedded cost model.

Invoice line-items are associated with contracts, and hence customers (clients and internal).

Invoices also produce revenues for each manager.

Client and Subsidy deliverables are billed at full cost with overhead. Ventures, internal, and overhead deliverables are billed at full cost without overhead. Once overhead is stripped from Client and Subsidy sales (to fund approved overhead deliverables), managers receive only the without-overhead rates for all sales, internal and external.

If revenues are to be received through fee-for-service, invoices trigger a transfer of money from a client's accounts to the internal service provider's.

If revenues are to be drawn from prepaid accounts, then invoices decrement the checkbooks carried within the internal service provider's accounts.

For services sold by one group to a peer within the organization (internal indirect costs), invoices recognize revenues on the seller side (just like sales to clients) and expenses on the buyer side (just like vendor costs).

For services sold by one group to the entire organization (overhead), invoices are billed to the overhead checkbook (which is replenished by stripping the overhead component of rates from revenues).

Invoices are not only a financial instrument. They tell clients what value they've received for their money. Invoices need to be understandable and believable, listing products and services delivered, by contract, and the costs of each.

An invoice approval (and perhaps adjustment) process ensures that clients are billed fairly.

Checkbook Accounting

To make the purchase-decision process meaningful, pursers have to know how much is in their checkbooks, as well as what the various potential deliverables cost.

The cost of deliverables is calculated at the beginning of the year in an investment-based budget. New projects and services that arise mid-year are estimated based on published rates. So costs are known. The next challenge is informing pursers of their checkbook balances.

If an organization receives revenues as a direct budget or via allocations, then checkbooks are established for these prepaid accounts.

In the case of direct budget, funding for Ventures and Subsidies is channeled into a checkbook that's owned by the organization itself. The remainder, typically the bulk of the budget, goes into a client-owned checkbook.

In the case of allocations, funding supplied by business units is placed in separate checkbooks which are owned and managed by each business unit independently.

For both direct budgets and allocations, the money is held in a special account. It's not distributed to the managers within the organization to cover their costs. It belongs to pursers, not the organization, until the organization earns it by delivering products and services.

If an internal service provider charges fee-for-service, then most checkbooks are maintained by clients within their normal enterprise accounting systems. Even then, there are some checkbooks maintained within the internal service provider's accounts: funding for Subsidies, Ventures, and overhead.

A checkbook for overhead (services agreed in the Planning process) is filled by stripping the overhead component out of revenues (from clients and Subsidies). Groups within an organization that provide overhead services then invoice this checkbook.

An accounting process maintains checkbook balances. Contracts may encumber funds, so that they're not spent twice. Then, once the work is delivered, invoices deduct prices from checkbooks (debits), and recognize managers' revenues (credits) which cover suppliers' costs.

Checkbooks may be metered over time, e.g., supplying pursers with 1/12th of their annual budget per month, to level demand.

Dashboards for Management and Clients

There's a lot of valuable data embedded in these various processes. The Actuals subsystem includes any reports, dashboards, and business-intelligence databases that might help managers within an internal service provider run efficient and effective businesses, and help pursers make wise purchase decisions.

Managers, first and foremost, need "profit and loss" (P&L) statements which describe their revenues and their expenditures.

* On one side of the report, they show actual costs by general-ledger expense-code — compensation, travel, training, vendor services, depreciation, etc.

* On the other side of the report, they show revenues by product and service.

* The net (revenues minus expenses) shows a variance from break-even.

The P&L statement is a key metric. Internal market economics does not condone traditional variance analysis, where managers are questioned if their expenditures exceed planned. Expenditures over planned may be legitimate, as long as revenues exceed planned in an equal amount. The proper managerial metric is the net of revenues minus expenses, the "bottom line" rather than the "top line."

The P&L statement also indicates which products and services, and which costs, are shrinking and growing. These data may indicate the need for deep-dive analyses of market trends and product profitability.

To produce a P&L, the enterprise's general-ledger system provides costs. Revenue data comes from invoices.

A P&L can juxtapose actual with planned revenues and expenses, perhaps simply by prorating the annual cost and revenue forecasts in the plan. If it's worth the effort, managers can be asked to forecast revenues and expenses for the remainder of the year to create a pro-forma P&L.

Another important metric is billable-time ratios — the percentage of total staff time spent on deliverables rather than indirect sustenance activities.

Other key managerial metrics, such as customer satisfaction and market share, may not be generated automatically by the Actuals subsystem. They may require special studies.

(For more on management metrics, see Chapter 15.)

For clients, dashboards focus on what they've bought. Clients may wish to see the details beneath the invoices they've received, or they may wish to aggregate invoice data to a higher level to see trends such as consumption by product or by groups within their organizations.

Optional Components

Once the six essential components are working, the following optional components enhance the effectiveness of an internal market economy:

Benchmarking

One optional component builds on the Planning subsystem to enhance organizational performance: benchmarking.

One of the most important metrics of an organization in an internal market economy is *value*. Value means quality in proportion to cost (distinct from benefits, which can only be measured by clients in the context of their specific uses of an internal service provider's products and services).

The simplest and most comprehensive and pragmatic way to measure value is benchmarking internal rates against alternative sources such as outsourcing. (See Chapter 13.)

Generally it's impossible to compare every rate in a catalog with external sources. Not all products and services are available from external vendors. Plus, a comprehensive study would be expensive and time consuming.

More practically, a subset of the rates can be selected for benchmarking. External prices can be logged in a database of benchmarks, which can be augmented and updated over time.

While based on Planning data, benchmarking becomes a continual process of gathering and updating external rates for comparison as entrepreneurs keep up with their external counterparts.

Automated Order Entry (Request Management)

Some portion of an internal service providers' revenues come from the sale of routine, commodity products and services — things that can be selected from a published catalog, without much help and without detailed contract negotiations. Pursers may not wish to be bothered by all these routine, small requests.

As a refinement to the client purchase-decision process, pursers may transfer a portion of their checkbooks into sub-checkbooks to fund commodity purchases. Pursers then define who is entitled to benefit from it, and what kinds of purchases it can fund.

(Of course, it's a fixed-sum game; money put in this sub-checkbook is no longer available for use by pursers on big projects and services.)

Once a sub-checkbook is established, internal service providers can set up an efficient process that allows clients to order commodities (within the specified entitlements). This may take the form of a web store — an "Amazon-like experience — and may even automatically dispatch orders to the appropriate groups within the organization. (In ITIL, this is termed "request management.")

This relieves pursers of having to look at the many small requests that are routinely approved, focusing their attention on more strategic investments. It makes it very easy for clients to place orders. And it makes order fulfillment more efficient.

However, note that automated order entry only facilitates the purchasing of commodity products and services, not of bigger and more strategic projects. That's why this is considered a refinement rather than an essential component of internal market economics.

ROI Analysis (Benefits Measurement, Total Cost of Ownership)

Throughout the year, pursers decide which products and services to buy with their checkbooks.

Of course, to rank their various investment alternatives, decision-makers balance costs against benefits. Ideally, they examine the ROI of each investment opportunity.

To calculate ROI, decision-makers need to know two things:

*   Total cost of ownership, which includes not only the initial investment but also operating costs throughout the life of the asset.

*   Benefits, including strategic benefits which some (mistakenly) refer to as intangible.

Based on the current year's rates developed in the Planning process plus some assumptions about cost trends, internal service providers can project total costs of ownership.

The benefits side of the equation is more difficult. But methods are available to help clients quantify both cost-displacement and value-added benefits, using well accepted financial and decision-science techniques. [57] With these methods, you can quantify the so-called "intangible" strategic benefits. It just takes some training and experience to measure them. And each analysis takes time.

In fact, client executives make pretty good judgments based on their intuitive understanding of benefits. However, if pursers would like additional input to refine their decision making, internal service providers can learn these methods and offer benefits-measurement facilitation as a service.

Even if ROI is calculated, it should always be remembered that numbers are an *input* to managerial judgment, not a replacement for it.

ROI calculations are far from precise. Measuring benefits requires estimates of quantities and value, analysis of the probability of various outcomes, and comparisons with the next-best-alternative. Projecting costs over the useful life of an investment involves more estimates. The interest rates at which future cash flows are discounted are based on the enterprise's weighted-average cost of capital, again an approximation.

Given all these estimates, projects which barely meet ROI thresholds are questionable. A slight change in an estimate such that they're over the threshold probably doesn't make them good investments.

Nonetheless, an investment in benefits measurement methods can contribute insights and enhance management judgments, improving financial performance.

Product/Service Profitability Analysis

A cost model is a necessary element of the Planning subsystem, used to produce an investment-based budget and to calculate the rates which are published in the catalog. But it isn't required in the Actuals subsystem.

The invoicing system converts utilization data into prices by multiplying actual utilization (volume) times *published* rates, and hence doesn't have to associate actual costs with products and services through a cost model.

Actuals systems also produce profit-and-loss (P&L) statements for each manager. Again, a cost model isn't needed. Revenues are by product/service. But costs are by expense-code — a standard view of spending straight out of the general-ledger system.

Consider the questions that can be answered so far with a cost model in the Planning tool but not in the Actuals systems:

*   You'll know whether spending is under control by looking at the net of costs and revenues (on the P&L).

*   If there are concerns, you'll know costs by general-ledger expense-code.

*   You'll know whether sales (delivery) meet the plan by looking at revenues per product/service (again on the P&L).

A cost model is not required to produce these key management metrics.

However, there is one benefit to building a cost model within the Actuals subsystem: It gives you the ability to continually monitor the profitability of specific products and services.

Invoicing gives you revenues by product/service (based on published rates). A cost model in the Actuals subsystem gives you actual costs by product/service. The difference is profitability by product and service.

Why would an internal service provider want to continually analyze the profitability of its products and services?

Generally, it's not for "cream-skimming" — deciding which products and services it will and won't offer. Most internal service providers strive to be the vendor of choice to their clients, and therefore must be full-service suppliers. And even if they wish to focus on profitable products, these decisions are generally made in the Planning process, not abruptly mid-year; they should be based on strategy, not on some costs drifting out of line.

And continual profitability analysis is not needed to decide which products and services to outsource. If published rates (from the Planning subsystem) are not competitive, then you may want to investigate sourcing alternatives. And if the P&L shows a negative net, then actual costs may be higher than published rates and you may want to look into cost-control measures such as a sourcing.

The only real value of continual product/service profitability analysis is to very quickly find targets for efficiency improvements — specific products and services that *suddenly* become unprofitable and need scrutiny.

And to be more specific, it's to find problems in *direct* costs. Indirect costs which affect multiple products and services are just as easily analyzed with a standard P&L statement.

Of course, there are other ways to achieve this same purpose without incurring the expense of building and maintaining a second cost model in the Actuals subsystem. When the net (revenues minus expenses on a manager's P&L) becomes negative, a focused analysis of that specific group is an efficient way to find out which costs are out of line.

But if this sort of focused analysis becomes commonplace, then it may be worthwhile to implement the second cost model in the Actuals subsystem. If you do so, there is one important caveat: It must precisely match the cost model in your planning tool. It would create confusion and gain no value if published rates are calculated with one cost model and actual results are analyzed with another.

Costs and Benefits

The Actuals subsystem, building on the Planning subsystem, completes the implementation of an internal market economy.

Clearly one major benefit is to make chargebacks (if any) consistent with the budgets and rates promised in the Planning subsystem. Beyond just that, it makes internal-economy processes dynamic throughout the year, as well as more accurate.

Implementing the Actuals subsystem typically requires new systems, as well as new governance processes. The component systems, with the data feeds that connect them, are listed in Appendix 5 and portrayed as a high-level architecture in Figure 6.

The costs of the Actuals subsystem are certainly justified by the benefits, both the problems avoided and the results delivered.

Over and above the problems solved by the Planning subsystem, the Actuals subsystem solves the remainder of Robert's problems described in Chapter 3:

* "You cost too much (for the value we perceive we get)."
* "My allocation is too big."
* "It's your money; do the best you can with it."
* "You're so bureaucratic."
* "You're the bottleneck!"
* "You're unreliable and incompetent."
* "I haven't got time to help on your project team."
* "You're not aligned with business strategies."
* "We need governance (in the form of a steering committee)."
* "Cut X percent."

Here are the benefits you can expect from the Actuals subsystem (described in Chapters 18 through 20):

*   Financial: Cost Savings, Level One — External Costs
*   Financial: Cost Savings, Level Two — Internal Costs
*   Financial: Cost Savings, Level Three — Demand Management
*   Financial: Optimal Allocation of Scarce Resources
*   Financial: Portfolio Management
*   Financial: Basis for Profitability Analysis
*   Relationship: Perception of Value Received
*   Relationship: Customers Control Their Purchase Decisions
*   Relationship: Allocations Under Client Control
*   Relationship: Managing Expectations
*   Relationship: Not an Obstacle
*   Relationship: Clear Mutual Commitments
*   Transformational: Internal Customer Focus
*   Transformational: Entrepreneurship
*   Transformational: Empowerment
*   Transformational: Integrity

The breakout of benefits associated with each component of the Actuals subsystem is contained in Appendix 6.

LEADERSHIP STRATEGIES

24. Implementing Internal Market Economics

This chapter helps you translate the two subsystems and their components into a practical implementation plan, and select the right person to lead the project.

Pilots

It's always wise to take things a step at a time. If you're contemplating an enterprisewide implementation of internal market economics, you may wish to pilot the concept in just one organization.

The ideal pilot organization is either a small business unit, or a large internal service provider. An organization of 100 to 2000 people is an ideal size for a pilot.

The pilot organization should not be a subset of an internal service provider, a group that must work closely with others to produce products and services for clients. For example, an entire IT department makes an excellent pilot; the operations group within IT is less appropriate because it is highly dependent on other groups within IT whose costs must be reflected in its rates.

Sequence

The two subsystems can also be implemented a step at a time. That leads to raises the question, which comes first: the Planning or the Actuals subsystem?

Some people think they have to get their historic data in good shape (Actuals) before they address the Planning subsystem. In fact, the opposite is true. It's better to put in place a business and budget-planning process *before* you implement portfolio management and product/service accounting. Here's why:

* **Planning *is* prerequisite:** You need a plan before Actuals data has analytic value (to compare actual results to a plan).

   Furthermore, accurate rates (from the Planning subsystem) are needed before meaningful invoices can be produced. Remember, invoices (in the Actuals subsystem) are calculated by multiplying actual utilization by *published* rates which come from the Planning subsystem.

* **Actuals *are not* prerequisite:** You don't need Actuals (historic) data to develop a plan. Initially, managers can use what they already know to produce reasonable plans. Actuals data then fine-tunes their judgment over time.

   Even if you already charge fee-for-service, the Actuals subsystem doesn't need to be perfected first. Invoices can be at planned costs until you're ready to improve their accuracy.

* **Quicker win:** Implementing a Planning process is relatively inexpensive and quick, with huge benefits. Implementing Actuals systems is more expensive (costly software, time to implement it, and behavioral changes like timecards), and has fewer benefits.

* **Save money sooner:** Planning takes costs out before they happen. Actuals reports identify cost-savings opportunities after the money has already been spent.

* **Have to do much of it anyway:** You'll have to do much of the Planning process anyway in the course of implementing Actuals systems, including decisions like lines of business,

your catalog and rate structure, a cost model, project codes, and definitions of unbillable time.

* **Motivation to change:** Until staff understand that they're funded based on the deliverables they sell (which they learn in the Planning process), they won't be interested in utilizing the Actuals data and they'll resist the administrative burden (e.g., timecards and contracting).

Do We Need an Enterprise Strategy First?

There's no need to wait for an enterprisewide strategic or business planning process before piloting internal market economics.

An enterprise strategy would help leaders generate ideas for new deliverables. But most leadership teams can readily forecast their potential sales, complete with some innovative proposals, without being given documented enterprise strategies.

And as for an enterprise business plan, again there's no need to wait. In fact, piloting investment-based budgeting is a good way to explore a new enterprisewide business-planning process.

When to Start

If you're ready to work on the Planning subsystem, your next question might be the timing.

There's no need to wait for the next budget cycle to implement a new Planning process. In fact, there are a number of advantages to implementing it mid-year.

A mid-year implementation replicates the current year's budget in the new tool and method — essentially "reverse engineering" the current budget. This allows managers to learn the process without the hard deadline of a budget submission due-date. It also allows them to tune the data to a known reality.

This mid-year recasting of the budget has the immediate effect of clarifying what's funded and what's not. This matches clients' expectations to available resources, and brings immediate relief on that issue. Of course, the amount of the budget won't be affected until the following year.

A mid-year implementation prepares an organization to do the following year's budget quite easily.

Implementation Phases

An expedient implementation strategy recognizes these prerequisites, and also delivers the major benefits quickly. Then, it evolves and improves processes over time. Consider five basic phases (summarized in Figure 4):

1. An effective strategy begins with the *Planning subsystem,* producing a business plan, an investment-based budget, and a catalog with rates. This alone delivers many immediate benefits, enumerated in Chapter 22.

    While an investment-based budget provides a businesslike basis for budget negotiations, once the size of the budget is determined, planned expenditures can be fed to accounting systems in the traditional format of general-ledger expense-codes by manager until the Actuals tracking systems catch up.

    This first phase delivers benefits quickly, for a reasonable initial investment. This helps gain the executive support that's needed for the next phase.

Figure 4: Recommended Implementation Strategy

1. Planning subsystem.
2. Client-driven purchase-decision process.
3. Accuracy of invoices.
4. Dashboards and revenue accounting.
5. Optional components.

---

2. Next, development of the Actuals subsystem begins by setting up a *client-driven demand-management process*. Four components are needed:

   Client purchase decisions (portfolio management): This is the key to making clients accountable for controlling their demand. Checkbooks are defined, along with pursers for each. Implementing this requires new processes, and a simple portfolio-management tool may be developed.

   Commitment tracking (internal contracts database): A contracts database is needed to drive invoicing.

   Invoicing: This can be a simple process at first. Until the necessary utilization-tracking systems are in place, invoices can be based on planned costs rather than on actual utilization where necessary. (Revenue accounting can wait for phase 4.)

   Checkbook accounting: At first, this can be based on a very simple (perhaps even spreadsheet-based) checkbook-management system.

   Again, this phase delivers significant benefits quickly. Clients understand that they must live within their means. They can adjust priorities dynamically throughout the year. And with clients making their own purchase decisions, internal service providers are no longer viewed as an obstacle or an adversary that has to be convinced of the merits of their requests.

These benefits pave the way for the larger investment that's required in phase three, and generates demand for the better data which results from that next investment.

3. Once these basic processes are operational, it's time to improve the *accuracy of the invoices* by linking the invoicing system to actual utilization data.

    The *utilization tracking* component is implemented in this phase.

    This includes time-reporting. In addition to implementing any necessary systems, staff are taught what's billable versus unbillable, and how to link their time to contracts.

    Investments in infrastructure-utilization metrics may also be required. In parallel, investments in asset management systems may be required to provide the configuration data that's needed to link infrastructure utilization to contracts.

    The enterprise's general-ledger system is linked to the invoicing system to provide data on reimbursable costs.

4. Next, mining the data helps clients and internal service providers better manage their resources. *Revenue accounting* and *dashboards* components are implemented in this phase.

5. Once the essential components are working, the *optional components* and links to *dependent processes* may be implemented for additional benefits.

Implementation Planning: The Planning Subsystem

For the Planning subsystem, implementation planning is mostly a matter of gaining the commitment of the leadership team, since the process itself is well defined (see Appendix 7).

In a workshop, leaders list the problems they hope to solve, and the benefits they hope to gain, through internal market economics.

These objectives are linked to the various resource-governance processes, revealing which must be addressed to solve their most pressing leadership concerns.

Generally, many of their concerns trace their root cause to the Planning subsystem. Reinforcing that this is the best place to start, discussion explores the interdependencies, explaining why the Planning subsystem must come before the Actuals.

The need for management involvement, and the amount of time required, is discussed next. (See Chapter 22.)

Hopefully, the result is a leadership team committed to implementing the Planning subsystem, and to being personally involved in each step of the process.

Implementation Planning: The Actuals Subsystem

Implementing the Actuals subsystem is more mechanical than the Planning subsystem, and doesn't require significant leadership-team involvement. Project planning is also more complex.

Most organizations have some pieces of internal market economics working in their current financial and resource-governance processes. Thus, the first step is an assessment of your current practices and systems. Using a detailed framework of the essential and optional components, this assessment explores what's working and what's missing from your current resource-governance processes. (See Appendix 8.)

Once gaps are identified, the next step is to define your desired end-state — your unique version of an internal market economy.

The gaps relevant to that end-state generate tasks that make up a project plan. Of course, the project plan includes communications with all staff and clients, and training for both staff and pursers.

Gap analysis, along with the benefits of each component (described in Appendix 6), are used to justify the next investment in internal market economics.

Selecting the Right Leader

How can you select the right leader to manage your implementation of internal market economics?

There are different levels of understanding of financial and resource-governance processes:

*   **Analyst:** operates the tools and performs the analyses in current processes.

*   **Cost-accountant:** spreads costs equitably to the business, often without an understanding of the economic impacts.

*   **Controller:** constrains costs on behalf of shareholders, personally taking on decisions that should be made by customers and internal entrepreneurs.

None of these are a good choice to lead your internal market economy implementation, although all may be valued members of the project team.

A good leader goes beyond all of these:

*   **Transformational leader:** designs healthy organizations that can succeed, with or without her.

As Gary Hamel said, "...leaders will no longer be seen as grand visionaries, all-wise decision makers, and ironfisted disciplinarians. Instead, they will need to become social architects, constitution writers, and entrepreneurs of meaning. In this new model, the leader's job is to create an environment where every employee has the chance to collaborate, innovate, and excel." [58]

The manager has his eye always on the bottom line;
the leader has his eye on the horizon.

Warren Bennis [59]

Remember, internal market economics is more about governance processes and the organizational ecosystem than it is about accounting. In many organizations, the right leader is more likely to be found in a planning function, with its future-oriented perspective and facilitative style, than in a more operationally oriented finance group.

Through internal market economics, transformational leaders can leave a legacy of dynamic organizational processes that control costs wisely, channel scarce resources to the best possible uses, and tap everybody's creative energy through empowerment while intrinsically guiding them to contribute to the success of the enterprise.

25. Internal Market Economics
Within a Larger Transformation Strategy

The concept of market economics is clear to most; we live it every
day in the real world. I hope you agree that applying these
familiar concepts inside organizations makes sense.

Internal market economics enables better-informed budget and
strategy decisions, aligns resources with enterprise strategies,
clearly defines individual accountabilities, installs a discipline of
frugality, enhances teamwork, and provides a realistic view of
product-line profitability.

Internal market economics enhances shareholder value is
enhanced. But it's more than that.... It's a visionary way to run
an organization. It frees the entrepreneurial spirit in people at
every level of an organization. This augments motivation and
creativity, empowers people to succeed, and makes internal service
providers not only a "vendor of choice" but also an "employer of
choice" — attracting and retaining the best talent.

---

*Intrapreneurship is not just a way to increase the level of
innovation and productivity of organizations, although it will do that.
More importantly, it is a way of organizing vast businesses so that
work again becomes a joyful expression of one's contribution to society.*

Gifford Pinchot III
Author, "Intrapreneuring" [60]

But as powerful as it is, internal market economics is certainly not
a panacea that alone creates a high-performance organization.

Elements of a Transformation

Internal market economics is just one element in a leader's transformation strategy toward a business-within-a-business organization. Two other organizational systems are also essential: [61]

* **Structure:** the organization chart and workflows.

* **Culture:** the values and behaviors common throughout the organization.

A healthy *structure* defines jobs by lines of business — what groups sell, not what they do — unlike traditional organization charts which are defined in vague terms such as roles, responsibilities, competencies, and processes. [62]

A healthy *culture* defines the specific behaviors that manifest customer focus, entrepreneurship, teamwork, cooperation, empowerment, integrity, contracts, quality, and risk. [63]

Two other organizational systems can later be used to fine-tune and reinforce a business-within-a-business organization:

* **Methods and tools:** augmenting the capabilities of groups, including "best practices" and cross-boundary processes.

* **Metrics and rewards:** dashboards (beyond those defined by internal market economics), and rewards (or consequences) for performance.

These five systems are interdependent. But as long as they're all designed around the business-within-a-business paradigm, they'll work in concert, creating an organizational ecosystem that sends consistent signals which reinforce entrepreneurship.

Transformation Strategy: Where to Begin

There's no "best" sequence in addressing the three primary organizational systems (internal economy, structure, culture). A well designed structure makes internal market economics easier to implement, and vice versa. Both improve culture; and a comprehensive treatment of culture makes internal market economics and structure easier and more effective.

Internal market economics is an excellent choice as the first step for many organizations. It addresses real and pressing problems. It has a powerful impact on the organization and its clients. And it leads to insights on structure and changes in culture which pave the way for subsequent transformation initiatives.

Even if you're not considering a major transformation, you can gain significant returns for a reasonable investment in just the first phase of an internal market economy: the Planning subsystem. It alone delivers bottom-line results while solving pressing resource-governance problems.

The business planning and budgeting process was
the best place to start running IT like a business.

Ralph Caruso
CIO
University of Maine [64]

With internal market economics, the path forward is well-defined. Implementation processes are tested and proven. And the benefits are real and profound. Applying the common sense of market economics to the resource-governance processes within organizations is a powerful leadership initiative.